Edward and Tyler
Relapse & Recovery

Other books by Edward Bear

The Dark Night of Recovery

The Seven Deadly Needs

The Seven Deadly Fears

The Cocktail Cart

Tyler and the Twelve Traditions

Edward and Tyler Relapse & Recovery

Edward Bear

White River Press
Amherst, Massachusetts

Acknowledgements:
For permission to use the following selections, grateful
thanks are extended:
Alcoholics Anonymous. New York. World Services, Inc.
1955. *Twelve Steps and Twelve Traditions*. New York.
World Services, Inc. 1952.

Cover by Sarah Edgell. sarah@edgellworks.com

White River Press edition published January 2015
White River Press LLC
PO Box 3561
Amherst, MA 01004
whiteriverpress.com

ISBN 978-1-935052-64-7 (paperback)
      978-1-887043-16-8 (ebook)

First published May 2006 by M&J Publishing, Denver, Colorado

Library of Congress Control Number: 2006923461

PUBLISHER'S NOTE
This is a work of fiction. Any resemblance to persons, living or dead, events, or locales is entirely coincidental.

The gem cannot be polished without friction, no man perfected without trials.
> Confucius

Unless a man has been kicked around a little, you can't really depend on him to amount to anything.
> William Feather

From errors and mistakes, the wise learn wisdom for the future.
> Plutarch

God will not look you over for medals, degrees or diplomas, but for scars.
> Anonymous

If there were no tribulation, there would be no rest; if there were no winter, there would be no summer.
> Saint John Chrysostom

You learn to walk by falling down.
> Chinese Proverb

Relinquishing control is the ultimate challenge of the Spiritual Warrior.
> The Book of Runes

The Twelve Steps of Alcoholics Anonymous

1. We admitted we were powerless over alcohol—that our lives had become unmanageable.
2. Came to believe that a Power greater than ourselves could restore us to sanity.
3. Made a decision to turn our will and our lives over to the care of God *as we understood Him.*
4. Made a searching and fearless moral inventory of ourselves.
5. Admitted to God, to ourselves, and to another human being the exact nature of our wrongs.
6. Were entirely ready to have God remove all these defects of character.
7. Humbly asked Him to remove our shortcomings.
8. Made a list of all persons we had harmed and became willing to make amends to them all.
9. Made direct amends wherever possible, except when to do so would injure them or others.
10. Continued to take personal inventory and when we were wrong promptly admitted it.
11. Sought through prayer and meditation to improve our conscious contact with God *as we understood Him,* praying only for knowledge of His will for us and the power to carry that out.
12. Having had a spiritual awakening as the result of these steps, we tried to carry this message to alcoholics, and to practice these principles in all our affairs.

To:

Jo, who puts the colors in all the rainbows.

The children: Tommy (wherever you are), Tree, Cat, Monica, Laura & Steven.

All those who have survived to teach us about the journey back.

PROLOGUE

Some days the dragon wins.
Anonymous

Yes, the rumors are all true. Yours truly, Edward Bear, Man-About-Town, Former Lush, had a relapse, a nightmare trip down Memory Lane. God…Twelve years into recovery and I picked up a drink, followed, of course, by quite a few more drinks. It talks about that in the Big Book, about an insane idea winning out over a perfectly rational one. Having a drink after twelve years in recovery certainly qualifies as an insane idea.

Don't ask me why because I don't think I have an answer. At least not yet. Tyler maintains that a relapse starts long before you pick up the drink. I think maybe, but I'm not convinced. Besides, Tyler's always coming up with some off-the-wall remark that's supposed to make him look like a genius.

At first, people thought I was kidding…*Not you, man… You're kiddin', right?* You could see the disappointment in their eyes, the doubt. And the fear. *Twelve years and he drank. If it can happen to him, it can happen to anyone. Who's next—Tyler? The Maestro himself?* Then, of course, comes the advice, the unsolicited, unwanted, totally useless advice from people who have never *had* a relapse (disguised as

1

questions because we don't really give advice) ...*What Step were you on?* Inevitably followed by...*How many meetings were you going to? Were you talking to your sponsor?* Yada, yada, yada...

I just wanted to scream at those people...*Haven't you been telling me it's a goddam disease? I don't need a reason to drink. I'm an alcoholic.*

Somehow Tyler figured out I was drinking long before anyone knew. I mean I never even saw him during the few weeks I was drinking, yet somehow he knew (it wasn't unusual for us not to see each other, especially when he was on the prowl over on the other side of town). Never had a drink outside my apartment; ordered it from Argosy Liquors and had it delivered. Clever, I thought. Communicated with very few people, those mostly in the morning when I was fairly coherent. Who did I think I was fooling? But Tyler knew. Don't ask me how, but he did.

Anyway, it's old news now. Pretty old. A few weeks, maybe a month. Well, not a month because Tyler made me promise to take a chip at my home group when I had thirty days. It'll be a month next Friday. Hallelujah...Thirty days. Big deal.

Twelve years in recovery. Good recovery, too, though in light of what happened, some might question that. Twelve years...And I picked up a drink.

Truth is, I'm scared to death. I have this façade, this manner that seems to say, I'm okay, I'm okay, I'm okay... how-are-*you*? But it's a front that's a mile wide and an inch deep. You get close to me and all my defense mechanisms kick in—the perimeter booby traps, the anti-personnel mines, the cynicism, jokes, anger, the whole arsenal. Because if you get too close you'll find out how really frightened I am. I can't have that. I'm in *The Impenetrable Fortress*, guarding against all intruders. Beware! The moat's filled with piranha fish and the drawbridge is up. And I'm shaking behind the castle walls.

One of Tyler's favorite themes is, We are without defense against the first drink. *And defense must come from what, Superman? Of course,* he said (he has this annoying habit of answering his own questions), *defense must come from a Higher Power, O Unenlightened One.*

And the worse thing? Having to raise my hand as a newcomer. But Tyler insisted that I do it.

Anybody here with less than thirty days?
I'm Edward and I'm an alcoholic…

Clap clap clapclapclap…Hooray for Edward.

Talk about ego deflation at depth. I had relative newcomers coming up and asking me if I needed a sponsor, young kids in their twenties and thirties doling out tired old AA cliches…If I hear *Keep coming back* one more time I'm gonna throw up. I'm going to *Keep coming back,* but if I had somewhere else to go, believe me, I'd go there.

You know, this is a lot worse than coming in as a newcomer. If you're new, really new, people are kind and solicitous and helpful. They can't do enough for you. If you're a retread, especially one who had some significant time in the program, you're treated with polite disdain, like maybe you've got some communicable disease and people don't want to get too close to you…Like, *Hi, Edward. Nice to see you. Gotta run, man. Give me a call…sometime.* And zip, they're gone, back to their old cronies, the ones who are safe and haven't relapsed. Yet.

3

Somewhere there's a definition of alcoholism as a... *chronic relapsing disease characterized by excessive consumption of alcohol.* So if it's a Chronic-Relapsing-Disease why does everyone treat me like I'm a leper? What I have, this chronic relapsing deal, is not contagious, folks. I'm not going to infect you with Relapse Disease. Actually I might even be able to help you by talking about my adventures (or misadventures) in the Research Unit of the Recovery Movement.

Tyler has suggested that I get over the self-pity part. He has this...thing he repeats all the time...*The only difference between a winner and a whiner is the sound of the "i."* He also has a Rule (I forget what number—Tyler has all kinds of Rules), that you only get three minutes to whine. He calls it Whine Time. Used to be longer, maybe six or seven minutes, but he's decided he doesn't have all that much time left to waste listening to people who just want to whine and not take some kind of action. Tyler's very big on the action part of the program.

If you expect to come in here, sit in the chair and get the message by Assmosis, you're mistaken. The equation is—No action equals no action. You're into the well-known zero-sum game. If you don't do anything, nothing is going to happen.

Anyway, I'm going to hook up with Tyler again, subject myself to the abuse and cynicism of the old man and see if we can't catch lightning in a bottle a second time. (He wants to do a book about it. Of course, *my* relapse, *my* humiliation, now he wants to publicize it so that everyone will know. Thanks, buddy.) Haven't seen him for a few days but Richard told me he'd seen him recently trying to crash the Hello Dolly meeting on the other side of town, pleading ignorance about not knowing it was a women's meeting. Fat chance.

More than likely looking for the Dowager Empress or some Cherry Creek Babe to ease his financial woes. Rumor has it that he's back playing the ponies. Another one of his many addictions. Not a good sign.

So how can a guy with that many character defects be seemingly plugged into a Higher Power? I mean he gambles, he shamelessly hustles the women, he still smokes, he borrows money and sometimes forgets to pay it back...God...

See, everybody thinks he's this spiritual giant who meditates for hours every day and is on more or less friendly terms with God as well as numerous lesser spirits. And, of course, with Father Thomas Keating, the wise old Trappist monk who lives up in Snowmass at the Benedictine Monastery. For some reason (and I have this on semi-good authority) Father Thomas actually likes him, likes Tyler. Thomas seems like such a perceptive guy, I can't imagine why he doesn't see through that flimsy act that Tyler puts on. More than likely it's a simple act of Christian charity, being kind to poor, misguided souls. Like Tyler.

Even with my admitted bias against things having to do with organized religion, I count Father Keating as one of the Good Guys. Most others I've met seem to be out riding the range trying to lasso lost souls and convert them to Christianity before they fall into the hands of other religious fanatics. I wonder sometimes if these people are getting frequent flyer miles for converts.

But Keating's not like that. He's very...ecumenical for lack of a better word. He would more than likely suggest that you honor your path, whatever that happens to be— Buddhist, Muslim, Hindu, Jew, etc. I think he's a genuine Holy Man, a title I don't toss around lightly (and one that he would certainly deny). Plus, he's the smartest guy I've ever met. Tyler says that, considering the crowd I ran around with, that's not surprising, intimating that I either ran around with a bunch of dummies or that there are just lots of people smarter than I am. But he's a lot smarter than Tyler, too. And Tyler, for all his failings as a person, is pretty smart.

Funny (well not really funny funny), but I had no intention of having a drink the night it all started. It was right after Samantha and I broke up; another marriage down the drain. A little over a year and it all went spiraling down the sink. I'm not fifty yet, or just barely fifty, and I've been married and divorced five times. Five times. Can you believe it? Out of the thirty or so years since I was old enough to even *get* married, I've had five divorces. Five for five. If it was a baseball line score, I'd be batting a thousand. Instead I'm hitting zero point crap. And I always go into these things with such high hopes. It'll be different this time. I know it will. Ho ho ho. I'm sure the Maestro will have some interesting things to say about it.

Anyway, it was at a party for old John. Twenty-nine years with Safeway. Twenty-nine years! He looked happy as a clam. Big grin with about half his teeth gone because the company cancelled dental insurance five years ago and he could never afford a dentist...I didn't have anything to do but sit home and feel sorry for myself that night, so I went. I mean I could've gone to the Old Kent meeting, but I'd already heard the speaker. And there was an open bar. I just walked up and said *Bourbon, seven, no ice*, like it was an everyday occurrence. Like I hadn't had over twelve years in recovery, like...like what? Twelve years without a drink. *Bourbon, seven, no ice*...Jesus. The insanity of it just blows me away. No mental defense against the first drink. Tyler says that if you're an alcoholic or an addict of any kind, there's no safe ground. You're always at risk. No matter how long you've been sober, you'll always be standing at the edge of the abyss. Not a comforting thought. And maybe I should have paid more attention.

I can't say that Tyler didn't warn me. Not in so many words, but you know how he is. He's not big on giving advice directly. He would suggest that a particular action might not be in my best interest. He might suggest I read a certain page in the Big Book, or the Twelve and Twelve, or something from Winnie the Pooh about the time they all got lost in the Hundred Acre Wood. When he's really out there, he's been known to recommend something from the Sixth Patriarch of Zen. He would take the indirect approach, hoping to get my attention without using a blunt instrument. Sometimes it works. Other times, I have to have it spelled out. Or get hit with the hammer. Tyler's not reluctant to use the hammer if necessary.

Romance and finance, he'd say, shaking his head, *the rocky shoreline where you keep running aground and sinking that leaky scow you're on.* (He was in the Navy during the Korean War, hence the allusions to the nautical world from time to time.)

He wondered (out loud, of course) if I knew that Samantha was twenty-five years younger than I was. Just wondered. Like maybe I didn't know that. What kind of question is that? I got very (righteously) indignant and defended my choice as one not dependent on age or looks. But then he always comes up with something stupid like, *Would you feel the same if she was fifty? Fifty-five maybe? And looked like Second-Hand Rose.* What does that have to do with anything? Why would I want to date somebody who

7

looked like Rose? Or somebody who was fifty-five. Tyler might, but then Tyler's seventy-two.

Anyway, I'm sure we'll get into all that before the sessions are done. It's the same drill as always. Bring the tape recorder, the pad, the pencil, be ready to do some reading and some writing. Evidently we're going to explore some of the less well known parts of the Big Book. Plus what he calls the Five Great Discoveries and the Two Great Fallacies. He mentioned the Ninth Step Promises, and his old favorite, Conditional Reality. Then there's the list of books that he wants me to read. I haven't even thought about any of it yet. It's like homework. I told him that when he suggested it, and he was quick to point out that the cover of the Big Book says that it's the basic text, as in textbook, as in going-back-to-school to study.

But Tyler gets pretty far afield. The list includes stuff like The Spirituality of Imperfection (which I've already read), The Dhammapada (a Buddhist text), Addiction and Grace, The Looking Glass Universe, Paradigms Lost, The Nature of Personal Reality, a book of poetry by Bukowski, tons more that I can't remember at the moment. When I protested about the cost of these items, he gave me that fish-eye look... *And what is your sobriety worth?*...Once again purposely misunderstanding my comment.

And though I love Tyler like a brother (or a father, though I didn't much love my own), I'm not looking forward to my meetings with him (which says more about me than it does about Tyler). I don't want to go through it again. I've got no wind in the sails. No gas in the tank. No mojo. I'm drifting at the mercy of whatever current seems to prevail. I don't see a shoreline—just the huge, angry sea wherever I look.

Horizon to horizon. I don't even have a compass. I have no idea which way I'm going. Or even *if* I'm going.

It's like the universe—there's no fixed point of reference. The earth seems to be spinning along on the outer limits of a galaxy we call the Milky Way, though nobody knows where we really are (in relationship to some mythical center), how fast we're going (is it 6,000 or 60,000 miles an hour?) or where we're going, or why we're going, or why we even evolved in the first place.

You remember that thing by Thomas Merton? That prayer? It was on a prayer card that I first found in church (long ago when I actually still went to church). Later I found it in recovery bookshops. It begins with something like... *Dear God, I do not see the road ahead of me. I have no idea where I'm going*, and ends with...*but I think the desire to please You does in fact please You. And I have that desire in everything I do.*

He wrote that after he'd been in the monastery for six or seven years. Maybe eight. All that time meditating, praying, working in the fields—(the monk's motto—to work and to pray) and he comes up empty. *What am I doing here, God? Where are You? Am I wasting my time here? Where the fuck are You?* (Please excuse the language. I get carried away sometimes.)

Tyler would suggest (and has) that the search for God (whatever that means to you) is just another form of greed, and though spiritual in nature, is the same greed that wants *things*—baubles, sex, money, security, etc. The key phrase in *I want God* and *I want a job* is *I want*. Just because you want something spiritual doesn't mitigate the greed factor. It's just another form of Conditional Reality that he's always harping on that says I'll be okay *If...*or I'll be okay *When...I find*

9

God. (So God's lost?) Which doesn't make a lick of sense to me. Then he always points out that the Big Book says that God could and would (relieve our alcoholism) if *sought...* not found. So (according to Tyler) it's permissible to seek as long as you realize that finding is the same as not finding. In other words, don't base your life on getting things, even spiritual things. How's that for twisted logic?

But I'm getting ahead of myself. We're set to meet next Thursday. He's coming over to my place, which is no great shakes but probably better than his. If he even has a place. We're still not sure. I'll have to get some good strong coffee (he's given up on decaf, heart trouble be damned) and some chocolate-covered peanut butter nuggets, his latest addiction, which he excuses because he says it's helping him quit smoking, though it hasn't yet. He now smokes and eats chocolate-covered peanut butter nuggets and drinks coffee, fueling every addiction known except alcohol. Almost every addiction. Hopefully, he's too old for other serious addictions. But we cut him some slack because he's been sober for thirty-seven years, so we figure he must have been doing something right.

Truth is (the rest of the book is the recorded conversations between the two of us so I have to get this in while I can), I'm terrified of the whole process. I don't know if I can do it, go through it again. And, though I haven't had a drink in over three weeks, I've had to fight it every day. It's not that a drink looks so good; it's that recovery looks so futile, so senseless. Life looks futile. A voice in my head keeps saying, *Why bother? You're the same jerk you always were. You just proved that to everyone who didn't already know. Look at stupid Edward...twelve years in recovery and he takes a*

drink. And hey, more than one, cousin. Wha'd you expect?
Loser, loser, still a boozer.

A drink would at least turn my head off for a while, quiet the voices. There's an old-timer who says that people shoot themselves in the head so they can be sure to turn off the voices.

What went wrong? Why, after all that time, did I take a drink? And perhaps the biggest question—Will I do it again? Can I get sober again? I'm told the statistics for people with double digit sobriety who go out and drink aren't good. Most don't make it back. That's not exactly true. Most (at least some) make it back but only briefly. Then they're gone for good. The next time we hear of them it's about funeral arrangements.

You know, last year about this time I had the world by the tail. I had entered the world of the Spirit. I had been catapulted into the fourth dimension (which a friend of mine calls the Fourth Dementia). All my work had finally paid off. I was so goddam proud of myself I could hardly stand it. And of course I had to tell everyone how spiritual I had become. But no sooner had I begun to bask in the glow of Divine favor when it all started to slip away. Ever so slowly, almost imperceptibly, the glow faded. I repeated endlessly, *I surrender, I surrender* …trying to retain some semblance of sanity, all to no avail. It took the better part of a year, but it's gone, and with it any real hope that it will return.

Why did it go? Where did it go? The Maestro says it's best to avoid most of the W words, like Why, When, Where and Who. And maybe How.

Tyler says we're going to talk about fear (I reminded him that we'd already done a whole book on fear and he said that fear was worth a couple of books), the historical roots of Step One, that other stuff I mentioned a couple of pages ago, and some general spiritual principles. I'm thinking, Bukowski? We're going to get spiritual principles from Charley Bukowski? *And you,* he said, meaning yours truly, *might be called upon to do some serious writing of your own.*

When I asked him if he wanted me to go through the Steps again he said, *Just Step One for now.* Which means, maybe we'll do the rest...later. Or maybe not. His usual evasive answer.

So here goes. This process saved my life once; maybe the magic will happen again.

CHAPTER ONE

You can steal my women, but don't play
with my whiskey.

Charles Bukowski

Tyler just had to make an entrance. I should have known. Thursday arrived and he came in with his Dodger uniform on, the one he got at Dodger Fantasy camp fifteen or twenty years ago. TYLER in big letters across the back. Number 35 below the name. The ever-present notebook under his arm (to neutralize that, I've got my own notebook, which I put on the table to be sure he'd see it). He's got the baseball pants, sanitary socks, stirrups, the whole outfit. Only thing that's missing is the baseball shoes. Tyler had his shower clogs on instead, which made the whole outfit look even more ridiculous. Plus it was wrinkled beyond belief. He could hardly wait for me to comment, so I acted like everything was normal, that I was really not at all surprised to see him in a Dodger uniform.

"Coffee?" I said.

He couldn't resist drawing my attention to the uniform.

"How do you like it?" he said, turning around so I'd get the full impact.

I tried to play it deadpan, but it was too much for me.

"…Tyler…"

"You realize, Edward, that this is from 1988, the year they won the World Series?"

"I had no idea," I said, flatly. "Wow…"

"You have absolutely no sense of history, Edward. None. I don't know how you've managed to live this long without acquiring some…historical perspective."

I thought it best to get him off the Sense of History track, which is one of his favorite complaints about the younger generation. Yeah, that's right, I'm fifty and he considers me one of the younger generation.

"Have a seat, Maestro. Relax. I'll get the coffee."

"Pants are almost too tight to sit down," he said, pulling at the waistband.

"They shrink?" I said.

"Must have," he said, ignoring the obvious fact that he probably weighs fifteen or twenty pounds more than he did in 1988.

"…So how've you been?"

He unbuttoned the top button on his pants and eased into the chair on the other side of the kitchen table.

"…Tolerable," he said.

"And Mercedes?" Mercedes is his Vampire companion.

"We're temporarily…not speaking."

"Anything serious?"

"She has accused me of various…things of which I am totally innocent."

"…Things?" I said.

"Yes…Things…But enough about me, Edward. We can talk about me anytime. The issue today is you and your relapse. How it happened, why it happened, and is it possible to regain some quality sobriety after such an event."

I got the coffee while he opened his notebook. He took a sip and pronounced it drinkable, which is a better response than I usually get. He began reading from the notebook.

"In the beginning," he said, *"God created heaven and earth. And the earth was without form and void; and darkness was upon the face of the deep."*

"The Bible?" I said.

"I believe that's from the Bible."

"...*That* Bible?"

"Yes...That one," he said.

"Why are we talking about the Bible? Why are *you* talking about the Bible?"

"I thought it was a nice touch. Give our readers something to think about. Something they wouldn't normally expect."

"A curve ball of sorts," I said.

"Very good. And apropos, considering my attire for the evening."

"Still doesn't answer the why question."

"I'm getting to that," he said. "And since you seem to be anxious to know why, I'll skip ahead to day six...On the sixth day, after everything else had been created, the animals, rats, horses, spiders, the vegetation, the oranges and kumquats and so forth, He created Adam and Eve, dropped them into the Garden of Eden, and told them to increase and multiply and fill the earth."

"They didn't seem to have any trouble with that part."

"True...People learned the fun part very quickly and got to be almost too good at increasing and multiplying. Actually we may have overshot the mark a bit. Then, on the seventh day, He pronounced His handiwork good, very good in fact, and took the day off."

"And I suspect He's been off ever since," I said. "Doesn't He know what's going on down here?"

"He may still be resting."

"Okay, why the Bible lesson? I mean the real reason."

"We're beginning at the beginning. Day One. *Darkness was upon the face of the deep.* The creation story. All was going well until He created a couple of people and set in motion the Greed Factor. Paradise lost. Then we arrive at Step One--the first lesson. The admission that we are powerless over certain substances and behaviors—that our lives had become unmanageable. The lesson you may have forgotten."

"Tyler..."

"Tyler what? You think we should start on Step Eleven, get your spiritual life in order, skip Step One and start damage control at some other level?"

"But we've done the whole thing to death, Tyler. You remember all the work we did on the Steps—Dark Night, The Seven Deadly Fears, The Seven Deadly Needs. We wrote books about them, for chrissakes."

"...Allow me to continue my digression to the Garden of Eden for now. We'll get back to the other stuff later."

I started to protest, but he just went on without missing a beat.

"So consider this...everything in the Garden of Eden is perfect. Darkness is no longer upon the face of the deep. Hallelujah. This is the real Paradise, not some sleazy Fantasy Island deal...You got any cigarettes?"

"I don't smoke," I said.

"I know you don't smoke. The question was, Do you have any cigarettes?"

"...I do."

16

"Do you think I could borrow one, perhaps even purchase one?"

"I may have an old pack of Salems somewhere. And why are you still smoking, Maestro?"

"...I'm hardly smoking at all," he said. "That's why I don't have any cigarettes. I rarely smoke. Only once or twice a week maybe. If that."

Rather than continue with this line of questioning, which I knew would be futile, I got him the Salems and an ashtray. He lit one and coughed for a good ten seconds.

"Ahhhh...That's better," he said. "So here was Adam in Paradise. Being the only person on earth he got lonesome, so God created a woman to be his companion. How about that for a nice friendly gesture?"

"But God," I said, "being all-powerful could have created a whole chorus line of foxy babes for him."

"Adam was new at the game. He had only been a person for a day, maybe only a few hours. So he didn't really know what to ask for. It's like when you're new to recovery; you don't know what's available. Plus, he was not yet greedy, as future generations have turned out to be. He had not yet discovered wine, or mead, or grog, or any of the alcoholic substances which turn some perfectly normal people into greedy pigs, whose rallying cry is, *I want more! I want more!*"

"The gimme group."

"Indeed...So now we have Adam and Eve, the progenitors of the entire human race, living in Paradise. There was only one provision that God made—*Don't eat the fruit of That Tree over there.*"

"A simple instruction," I said.

"Right. They could have had room service but there were no rooms yet. But they had absolutely everything they'd ever

17

need. They could spend their time trying to figure out how to increase and multiply. What more could they possibly want?"

"They're in Fat City."

"Indeed," he said. "What's the first Deadly Need?"

"Eh...Let me think. Don't tell me."

"Not to worry," said Tyler. "I have no intention of telling you."

"...The first Deadly Need is The Need to Know."

"Bravo, Star Pupil. And the tree whose fruit they were forbidden to eat?"

"The Tree of Knowledge?"

"Good," he said. "So here they are living in Paradise where everything is provided, though some ancient manuscripts suggest that Eve was already thinking of redecorating. They can just lounge around and spend some quality time trying to figure out how to increase and multiply."

"The good life...But not for long?"

"Not for long. They had only enjoyed the good life briefly before the grim specter of *More* reared its ugly head. Addicts always want more. Addiction, in all its forms, is a disease of more. There's never enough of anything. So, recognizing an opportunity when he sees one, The Serpent, the very first Connection, comes along and says, *Eve, baby, God doesn't want you to eat the fruit of that tree because if you do your eyes will be opened and you'll be just-like-God. Look at all the shit He created. Wouldn't you like to be able to do that?* The Power Trip Ploy, actually perfected in the Garden of Eden."

"And Eve goes for it," I said.

"She does. She eats one of the Let's-Get-Smart apples, gives one to Adam who eats it and immediately wants another one, because he thinks, even after only a few days

18

on the planet, that More Is Better. Before he can gobble it down, they hear the voice of God and they run off and hide. But God, who doesn't have anything better to do because there weren't a lot of people or problems yet, finds them in a few minutes and wants to know what's going on because He noticed that The Tree seemed to be missing a few apples."

"Caught red-handed."

"Adam immediately tried to lay it off on Eve, thereby setting a precedent for centuries to come. *She gave it to me* ...Then makes it even worse by trying to lay a little guilt trip on God...*The woman that you gave to be with me gave me the fruit*...Suggesting that Eve is damaged goods. He's now blaming Eve *and* God."

"Not a good thing. But of course, God's not fooled."

"Not for a minute," said Tyler. "And here we enter the penalty phase of the trial. He lays a heavy burden on Eve about sorrow and childbirth and tells her that Adam, though an absolute weasel for trying to blame everybody else, shall rule over her. And although Adam gets his share of the guilt, and is now going to have to work for a living, the last part of the sentence appeals to him. The Guys Rule part. That made up for a few other things."

"Hurray for God."

"Smart move for the guy who wrote it," said Tyler.

"Obviously not a woman."

"Obviously. That's why God is referred to as He."

"Well, Maestro, before we get too far afield, I hope you're going to explain how all this ties into Step One and my relapse."

"We're just reviewing the history of Step One, tracing it into antiquity. You remember—historical perspective."

"But..."

"You see, the powerlessness over certain behaviors and substances goes back to the beginning of time. It's not a new deal. We've been dealing with it for centuries."

"And you think Adam and Eve were not only the first people, but also the first people who needed to be in recovery?"

"Of course. Here they are living in Paradise, not a worry in the world and all they had to do in order to live there forever, rent free, was not eat the fruit of one lousy tree. Just one tree. There were probably hundreds of trees in Paradise. Lollipop Trees, Pear Trees, Cigarette Trees...You remember the song?"

"I do...The buzzing of the bees in the Cigarette Trees."

"That's the one," he said. "So they were in a Step One position—powerless over the compulsion to eat the forbidden fruit. And soon after ingesting the Smart Apple, their lives became truly unmanageable. They were booted out of Paradise to dwell in the Land of Nod, on the East of Eden. Notice the reference to the Land of Nod? The sly innuendo about drug addicts being on the nod."

"Could you be stretching things to make a point, Maestro?"

"Not a bit," said Tyler. "You'll see. Not only were they the first people who needed to be in recovery, they were also the first dysfunctional family. The two nutty parents and the two kids: Cain and Abel. And it came to pass..."

"Very biblical."

"...that Cain and Abel both brought offerings to God, who, for some unknown reason, had respect for Abel's offering and none for Cain's. So Cain, being the forerunner of all the Mafiosi to come, killed his brother because ...he got no respect."

"Tyler..."

"No, wait...Then things get even worse. Cain then marries some woman who just appears out of nowhere and the whole thing snowballs. People all over the planet were beginning to learn how to increase and multiply."

"It may have been something of a mistake that God made the increase and multiply part so enjoyable."

"True," said Tyler. "They even had to have a Flood to slow things down."

"And here we are in the twenty-first century, still pretty well screwed up."

"Seems so...You know that about thirty-five percent of the people in the U.S. die prematurely because of some kind of addiction—alcohol, drugs, tobacco, food, sex...well, maybe not sex."

"Don't underestimate the Jealous Husband Factor."

"And," said Tyler, "since there are about two and a half million people in this country who die every year, that means around eight hundred thousand people die a few months or a few years ahead of time."

"And you think it all started with Adam and Eve?"

"I do. And there may have been others."

"So who else do we have at the dawn of civilization who needed to be in recovery?"

"It's no secret," he said, "that Buddha himself recognized the problem early on. The first Noble Truth is *Ouch!* life hurts. You remember the second Noble Truth?"

"I do. *Ouch* is caused by craving."

"And the third?"

"*Ouch* is eliminated by overcoming craving."

"Very good," said Tyler. "And how do we do that?"

"Action, Zen Master. Action through the Buddhist Eight-fold Path."

"Excellent. And you did it without having to refer to your notebook."

"Which is more than I can say for you."

"Old age has taken its toll on my few remaining memory cells. But now the critical question: How do people in the recovery community overcome this craving?"

"More action—The Twelve Steps. So when do I graduate?"

"You may not have been paying attention, Edward. First of all, this is education without graduation. Second, just recently you failed the most important test—Step One, the Step that assures us that we are powerless over alcohol and that our lives had become unmanageable. Who was it that said, *Those who don't remember the past are doomed to repeat it?*"

"…Elizabeth Taylor?"

"Good guess but probably not accurate. The Buddha says in the Dhammapada that he is the sum of everything he has ever thought. Actually he says that our life is shaped by our mind; we become what we think…"

"Who cares what Buddha said."

"…*and* the Big Book reminds us that…*the main problem of the alcoholic centers in his mind rather than in his body*… So we try to trace the roots of the thought process that leads to the first drink. You remember where it talks about the peculiar mental twist whereby a totally insane idea wins out over a perfectly rational one?"

"I do."

"Give me an example."

"The jaywalker from the Big Book…and the guy who thought a little scotch in his milk would be okay…"

"From personal experience," said Tyler.

"That's harder."

"I know."

"Well...the idea that I could have a drink and not pay a substantial price for it. The idea that it was okay to order a bourbon, seven, no ice, and somehow escape the consequences. The idea that I could even have a drink."

"A slip starts long before you take the first drink," he said.

"I've heard that," I said. "From you actually."

"I want you to write about it, about what you were thinking when you walked up to the bar and said *Bourbon, seven, no ice.*"

"...I don't know what I was thinking. Doesn't it say somewhere in the Big Book that if you ask an alcoholic why he took that first drink, he has no more idea why than you do."

"The Big Book was written when nobody had any extended period of sobriety. After eleven years..."

"Twelve."

"Okay...After twelve years, doing the Steps a number of times, practicing the principles, I have a hunch you know why you picked up a drink."

"Honest to God, Maestro, I don't have a clue."

"Well, get the writing utensil and the paper out and see if your hand knows why...By the way, what did you forget?"

"What do you mean, What did I forget?" Tyler can be so irritating sometimes.

"Did you forget you were alcoholic? Did you forget you were powerless over alcohol? Did you forget that your primary purpose was to stay sober and help other drunks? Did you forget to go to meetings?"

"...That goddam Murray only goes to one meeting a week, Tyler. One. That upscale Beverly Glen meeting, which is not really a meeting at all. More like a social club. And he stays sober."

"Let me state the obvious—You're not Murray."

"You're saying I'm sicker than Murray," I said.

"No, you're saying that. But Murray may not have suffered the considerable damage that you did before embarking upon his own personal Road of Happy Destiny. Maybe he only needs one meeting a week...So you cut down on your meetings?"

"...A little."

"That's clue number one for all the detectives reading this," said Tyler. "What's the worst thing you can say about an alcoholic?"

"We've been over this...The worst thing you can say about an alcoholic is that he or she is really bright."

"Bright guys think they can figure-it-out. It's not figure-outable."

"Nice word," I said.

"It has possibilities...And the sentence from the Big Book that supports that contention?"

"I haven't memorized the Big Book yet, but it goes something like...The alcoholic, with hardly an exception, will be unable to stop drinking on the basis of self-knowledge."

"...*Absolutely* unable to stop drinking, indicating that being smart doesn't help...So we'll start there and see where it leads. Among other things, we'll investigate the Two Great Fallacies, which are...Edward?"

"You think I remember all that stuff?"

"Break out the notebook and I'll refresh your memory."

I've probably got the information somewhere, but...I did as I was told and opened my notebook.

24

"The Two Great Fallacies are," said Tyler, "Number one—*If enough people think I'm okay, I must be okay*...You get that?"

I nodded yes.

"And the second is, *If I can't figure out how it can happen, it can't happen.*"

"...Got it. Don't limit the *Is*, eh?"

"Indeed," said Tyler. "The age of miracles is still with us. Then we're going to explore The Five Great Discoveries. Which are...One—*My way doesn't work*. Two—*God has in store for me much better things than I have in store for me*. Three—*Action is the magic word.*"

"Slow down."

"Okay.....Four—*Life works from the inside out*. And Five—*The more I rely on my Higher Power, the more reliable It becomes.*"

"Those are the Five Great Discoveries?"

"Those are mine. Everybody has their own. I just happen to have them written down because if I don't write them down, I never remember."

"I remember one of your rules...If it's not written down, it's not real."

"Right...So we'll meet again in two weeks?"

"Your call, Maestro."

"No, better make it one week. And don't forget the Ninth Step Promises."

"I'm writing as fast as I can. Where are the Ninth Step Promises?"

"...In the Big Book."

"And just where in the Big Book, O Wise One?"

"Try the bottom of page eighty-three."

"And the part about self knowledge availed us nothing?"

"That's half *measures* availed us nothing. There are four references to self-knowledge in the Big Book. Part of your assignment will be to find them."

"All four?" I said.

"Yes, all four. A hint...They're all in the first fifty pages."

"One week?"

"One week."

"That's not much time."

"In your case, it doesn't seem wise to wait. Plus, I want you to call every night between nine and ten. If I don't answer, leave a message."

"You never answer your phone at night."

"I know. But that doesn't mean you shouldn't call."

"...I don't get it," I said.

"Not necessary to get-it," he said. "Only necessary to do-it."

"See you in two weeks."

"One week."

"Right. One week."

CHAPTER TWO

The race is not always to the swift, nor the
battle to the strong—but that's the way to bet.
Damon Runyan

"You playing the ponies again, Maestro?"

Sometimes I start out by trying to put him on the defensive.

"A week just flies by sometimes, doesn't it," said Tyler. "Especially when you've got an assignment that you might not have taken the time to do."

"Actually, Maestro, I wasn't completely clear on the assignment. I mean I don't recall anything specific. Anything …concrete."

"As I recall, Evasive Student, we were discussing the part of the Book that talks about the alcoholic being unable, *absolutely* unable, to stop drinking on the basis of self-knowledge. And I said, *We'll start there and see where it leads.* Later I mentioned the number of times the Big Book alludes to self-knowledge and asked you to find the references, four in number if I recall correctly. Then you said…"

"How do you remember that stuff? I bet you can't remember what you had for breakfast this morning?"

"I have the same thing for breakfast every morning, Edward. You know that. Three Tylenol, a couple of stool softeners, and a bowl of High Fiber Raisin Branflakes."

"Perhaps that wasn't a good question. How about lunch?"

"Ah, lunch," he said, shaking his head. "I'm a little vague about lunch."

"Yet you remember our conversation from a week ago."

"You remember things according to their importance, Edward. That's why Holocaust survivors remember conversations from sixty years ago."

"I hardly think our conversation had that kind of importance."

"Holocaust survivors talk about survival, Edward. And what was our conversation about last week?"

"Relapse," I said. "…A slip. Taking a drink."

"Our conversation was about survival. I don't think of it in terms of drinking or not drinking. I think of it in terms of living or dying. Survival."

"Well…"

"Did you have a good time when you were drinking?"

"…Maybe for about fifteen minutes. After the first rush I looked at myself in the mirror and thought, O my God, what have I done?"

"And the feeling?"

"…Despair…I just wanted to disappear."

"Suicide?"

"Oddly enough, I don't think I was suicidal. I just didn't want to be anymore. You ever feel that way?"

"I have," said Tyler.

"Being, just be-ing was too much. I wanted out. It's an old feeling that I used to have all the time. A feeling that went away after a few drinks."

"The alcohol cure."

"Yes…But sometimes, when I think about dying, I'm afraid I'll just be…somewhere else. That there's no escape. I'll be trapped on this endless, claustrophobic, wheel of death and rebirth for all eternity. That I'll be just as crazy and afraid as I've always been and now there's no way out because something in me, my soul or my personality, something, is going to live forever. Maybe Sartre was right. Maybe there really is no exit. The Voices and the Demons will never go away."

"The idea that it could be different doesn't occur to you?"

"Rarely…When I think about my exit strategy, my best case scenario is going to sleep surrounded by people who love me unconditionally."

"A possibility."

"…Then I wake up on the Other Side sitting on a nice soft cloud with an easy-to-play harp. Maybe an instructional book by Mel Bay—Easy Hymns For Neophyte Angels. Then of course my first meeting…*Anybody been an angel for less than thirty days?* And I raise my hand as the other angels clap. I can play Beatles songs for eternity and not think about anything. My head will finally turn off. At last—freedom. If there is such a place as Heaven, that's probably what it's like—no more thinking. No more attacks by the Voices and the Demons. But like all those things that indicate there might be some hope, some place of rest and ease and comfort, it vanishes quickly and the old fears return."

"What are you afraid of?" said Tyler.

"…Everything…It's just a nameless terror. I'm drowning. I'm suffocating. Somebody is stuffing old paint rags in my mouth and setting them on fire."

"That ever happen?"

"I don't know. But I have dreams about it. Living forever is not a comforting thought, Maestro. What occurs to me when I'm in those dark places is that it's always going to be like this. To the grave...and beyond. I won't even have death to look forward to."

"So what do you do? You try to figure it out?"

"Sometimes. And sometimes I actually do the right thing and turn my thoughts to someone I can help. I pick up the fifty-pound phone and talk to another alcoholic, ask them how *they* are."

"...And?"

"And the feeling of despair seems to go away and I'm okay for awhile."

"...Until?"

"Until my mind rushes back to pick up this thread of fear that weaves its way through my life. I don't even know the right questions to ask. My mind has a mind of its own. It's like picking up a cobra and playing with it. Very dangerous, but somehow I can't help myself. *Nice cobra, don't bite Edward*...I'm stuck with the notion that I can actually figure it out, that I can intellectually surround these mysteries that we live with, and by sheer force of will figure them out."

"And then you'll be safe," said Tyler.

"Exactly. And then I'll be safe. No more fear. Because if I can just find the right question, maybe, just maybe, I can find an answer that I can use when the fear and despair reappear in my life. I was never afraid like this when I was drinking."

"Odd," said Tyler, "the things we remember about drinking."

"Well I wasn't."

30

"But you don't think picking up the phone and talking to another alcoholic is the answer? At least one answer?"

I have to be careful because Mister Innocent lays these verbal traps for me and before I know it I'm stuck admitting something I don't actually believe...Just because it's logical.

"It's so...lame, Tyler. Pick up the phone and talk to another alcoholic. What happens when I hang up? More fear. Then I have to call somebody else. I'll be on the phone day and night. Doesn't that sound ridiculous?"

"No. And as an added bonus, it works."

"Well..."

"The first mention of self-knowledge occurs on page seven in the..."

"Tyler...I'm talking about real stuff here. Don't get me sidetracked."

"We just crashed and burned on the intellectual level, Edward. I'm trying to get us away from the wreckage while there's still time."

"But we can return to it later? To this discussion?"

"If you insist. But possibly when we get through a few more sessions there will be no need to revisit the subject. For the present, let us move on with the current topic. We will try not to confuse our readers more than is absolutely necessary."

"I'm adopting a wait-and-see attitude," I said. "And it may surprise you, but I *do* know some of the references from the Big Book concerning self-knowledge."

"Commendable," said Tyler. "As I was saying, the first reference takes place following Bill's release from yet another hospital after undergoing the belladonna treatment..."

"They did drug treatment then?"

"There was little else they could do. He underwent hydrotherapy, drug therapy, did some exercises and met a wise old doctor…"

"I bet it doesn't say wise and old in the Big Book. Not together like that."

"Actually it says a *kind* doctor, but I thought I'd embellish it a little and put wise and old together so you'd get the picture about age and wisdom."

"I saw right though your flimsy scheme."

"What a keen mind you have, Edward. But to continue …This doctor explained to Bill that he had been seriously ill, mentally and physically, but that now, since he had been treated and gained all this information about his condition, he was well."

"Ho ho…"

"Correct. Here's what Bill says…

Understanding myself now, I went forth with high hopes. For three or four months the goose hung high. I went to town and even made a little money. Surely this was the answer—self-knowledge…

"I like that—*The goose hung high. For three or four months, the goose hung high.* Sounds like something out of Dickens. You don't hear that kind of language anymore. But of course self-knowledge wasn't the answer."

"No," he said. "It seldom is."

"I am now going to impress you with a quote about self-knowledge. Which, if you remember, I paraphrased last week when we talked about sobriety not being figureoutable."

"I'm ready. Impress me."

"...The actual or potential alcoholic, with hardly an exception, will be absolutely unable to stop drinking on the basis of self-knowledge."

"Well done. And it goes on to say that this is a point they wish to emphasize and reemphasize, to smash home to our readers as it has been revealed to us by bitter experience."

"Strong words," I said. "Smash home...bitter experience. But isn't self-knowledge supposed to be a good thing? Didn't the ancients believe that? What does the Oracle at Delphi say—Know Thyself?"

"Right," said Tyler. "We need to make a subtle distinction here. When they use the term self-knowledge in the Big Book, I believe they're referring to our knowledge about the disease of alcoholism. And as they discovered, knowing a lot about alcoholism doesn't mean I can stop drinking. It just means I know a lot about alcoholism."

"But maybe a certain amount of self-knowledge isn't all that bad," I said. I hate to let him off the hook so easily. "What about that searching and fearless moral inventory... of ourselves?"

"You know, Edward, there are days when just talking to you gives me a nosebleed."

"Glad I haven't lost my touch."

"I'm trying to point out the difference between self-knowledge and the ability to quit drinking. The two are not related."

I put on my most Puzzled Expression. Which, I know, really yanks his chain.

"See the difference?" he said.

"Well...I see some difference, but I'm not sure how clear I am about it. We might be comparing two different things that don't have anything to do with each other. You know, like apples and oranges."

"It's all in Step Four...*Being convinced that self,* not self-knowledge, Edward, *self...manifested in various ways, was what had defeated us, we considered its common manifestation.*"

"The common manifestation being resentment," I said, hoping to salvage a few points from the exchange.

"Bravo," said Tyler. "Resentment, the thing that destroys more alcoholics than anything else."

I scribbled in my notebook.

"...Do conversations like this tire you, Edward?"

I stopped pretending to write in my notebook for a moment.

"...Sometimes," I said cautiously.

"Me, too," he said, taking a deep breath and exhaling slowly. "So let's move on to Fred. You remember Fred, of course."

"...Of course. That's Fred...in the Big Book?"

"The same Fred, who ends up in the hospital with a bad case of jitters due to his drinking, but convinces himself that the experience, plus all the knowledge he has gained about his condition—repeat, Edward, all the knowledge he has gained about his condition—is all he needs to straighten out and stay sober."

"Self-knowledge equals sobriety?"

"Something like that," said Tyler. "But surprise, surprise, shortly after his release he began drinking again without any thought of the consequences."

"Bourbon, seven, no ice."

"Precisely...He discovered that...*Will power and self-knowledge would not help in those strange mental blank spots.* You see, he knew about alcoholism, had some knowledge about his condition, but still ended up taking a drink. Defense must come from where?"

"From a Higher Power...Unless one doesn't believe in a Higher Power. Then defense comes from where, O Wise One?"

"Are we going to go back to revisit the God thing?" said Tyler.

"The God thing is very important. You said so yourself."

"What did Augustine say?"

"...About belief?"

"About belief."

"He said, *I believe Lord. Help Thou my unbelief.* He also said, *O God grant me chastity...but not yet.*"

"Remember the part that goes...*Do I now believe, or am I even willing to believe...*"

"I do."

"Well, it's like that," said Tyler.

"*What's* like that?"

"Belief. You only have to be willing to believe. *Acting as if* has a long and honorable spiritual tradition."

"We're back to the Pollyanna tradition of hypocrisy and deceit. Supported by the worst slogan in AA—*Fake it till you make it.*"

"No, we're back to suspending your current, faulty belief system so that this Higher Power can work in your life. And while you're at it, stop finding ways to sabotage yourself."

"But..."

"Your way doesn't work, Edward. Remember the First Great Discovery: *My way doesn't work...*Get that through your head. Never has, never will. If you're going to survive, which I'm not at all sure of at the moment, I suggest you lose about thirty points off your IQ. That way you might stand a chance. Might."

"Why are you getting all worked up?"

"Because if you don't start listening, you're going to walk out the door and begin a slow agonizing slide into insanity and death. I love you too much to want to see that happen. I watched my father die like that. And my oldest son. Not a pretty sight. You're too goddam cavalier about this relapse. We can play word games or we can get honest about what's going on."

"That's just me, Maestro. You know that. The more scared I get, the funnier I try to be."

"You remember when George went to treatment and tried his stand-up comedy routine?"

"Yeah."

"And they put him on joke restriction because he was using humor to avoid real issues."

"You think I do that?"

"Oh, yes."

"Being funny," I said, "is not the same thing as being evasive."

"In your case, it is," said Tyler. "...But enough for tonight. We shall put it away for now and focus on next week."

"I'm eagerly awaiting my assignment," I said.

"Your assignment is to explain what the First Great Fallacy means."

"*If enough people think I'm okay, I must be okay*? That it?"

"That's the one," said Tyler.

"You want me to explain it to you?"

"I do...And if that doesn't occupy your time, you might let me know how many times self-pity is mentioned in the first hundred and sixty-four pages."

36

"You want me to count them?"

"Yeah...Unless you know another way of finding out."

"I'm still a little scattered."

"I'd call that a normal reaction after a relapse."

"But I took my thirty-day chip."

"I heard," he said.

"And I absolutely hated it. Everybody clapping, whooping it up. You know how my home group is. It's like a high school pep rally. Seven o'clock in the morning and everybody's so... up. It's disgusting. And I bet there were people in that room who were glad I relapsed."

"I doubt that. But if there were, I would suggest you let it be their problem."

"I know, I know," I said. "Serenity Prayer issue. God, Tyler, I don't know if I can do this again."

"You can."

"I don't know if I believe that."

"Do you believe that I believe?"

"...Yeah."

"That's enough for now. See you next week."

CHAPTER THREE

I fled Him down the nights and down the days;
I fled Him down the arches of the years...
                        The Hound of Heaven
                        Francis Thompson

"You had a better week?" said Tyler.

"I did. For one thing I didn't spend the whole week thinking about Samantha. That in itself gave me some relief."

"I wonder why we think that concentrating on a problem will make it go away."

"You mean it doesn't?" I said.

"No."

"So how are we supposed to solve a problem?"

"You turn it over," he said.

"And then...?"

"Then you wait, admittedly not one of our strong points"

"How long do you wait?"

"Till it gets resolved."

"And if it doesn't?" I said.

"Oh, they all get resolved...eventually," he said.

"Ah, the old Eventually Ploy. Is that like God answers all your prayers but sometimes the answer is No?"

"It's more like your Higher Power or your Higher Self or the Great Pumpkin knows exactly what you need, so you only have to present the problem, get out of the way, and let it spin out against the backdrop of time."

"This is like a fairy tale, right?" I said. "You present your problem to the Wizard and he figures it out? Or delegates a few Trolls to work on it?"

"That's closer than you might think. One of the great gifts of the program is the willingness to live with unresolved problems. I don't have to know all the answers today."

"Sounds like a copout," I said.

"Not so."

"...I'm not sure I believe that...Anyway, moving along with last week's lesson, self-pity is mentioned ten times in the first hundred and sixty-four pages of the Big Book."

"You counted them?"

"Actually, Trucker Bill told me."

"*He* counted them?"

"...Must have, Tyler. How else would he know?"

"Pilot John could have told him. Anybody. Most people we know can count. At least up to ten."

"Why do you always insist on complicating things, Maestro? It was just a simple statement—self-pity is mentioned ten times. Does it make any difference if it's nine...or eleven, or twelve?"

"No. But it's actually eleven."

"And of course you've counted them."

"Of course," he said.

"You know, that's a totally anal thing to do. I can't imagine how drab and empty your life must be when you're reduced to counting words in the Big Book for entertainment. Clue, Maestro—nobody cares how many times self-pity is mentioned."

39

"But we do, Edward. You and me. Because if you had really counted them, you would have at least had to scan the text, maybe even twice to get the right number. You might even have picked up some information you had previously missed."

"...But that was for extra credit, right? I mean you said if I had time."

"True," he said.

"So I don't get any demerits because it wasn't included in the assignment."

"We're not working on the merit/demerit system, Edward. If you stay sober, you pass, if you don't, you have to take the course again. And there's only one basic course—the core curriculum consisting of the Twelve Steps."

"The foundation you always talk about."

"Right," he said. "And if the foundation is good, you can build a mansion on it."

"A castle?" I said.

"If the foundation is solid you can build anything you want on it. Some would insist that you have to live in the basement, but that's not true. Just be sure you go down there from time to time to check the structural integrity."

"I could build a music room...and a research room."

"A research room?" said Tyler.

"A big bedroom."

"Figures."

"...Did I fail because I had a relapse?"

"Well," said Tyler, "although I sometimes use it, I don't really like the word fail. I like to think of it as a temporary setback, which, if you're willing, need only be temporary. Ali said it best—*Ain't nothing wrong with goin' down. It's staying down that's wrong.*"

40

"Ali the fighter?"

"The same," said Tyler. "Edgar Cayce said it, too, *You just keep coming back till you get it right*...Now on to the lesson."

"*If enough people think I'm okay, I must be okay.*"

"That's the one."

"And you wanted me to tell you what it means," I said.

"Right."

"Since it's your discovery, shouldn't you be explaining it to me?"

"I thought we might find some common ground here. Perhaps a sense of identification with the sentiment."

"I thought a lot about it...And I took some notes."

"Notes are allowed," said Tyler. "Would you care to read some of them?"

"They're not very...coherent."

"Not necessary they be coherent, Edward. Just reach right in there and grab a word, any word, and we'll start from there."

"How about approval. If enough people approve of me, it means I'm okay."

"And if they don't?"

"I'm not okay."

"And if you're not okay, what are you?"

"...A failure?"

"Maybe...How do you get okay?"

"Get everyone's approval?"

"My turn to ask the questions," said Tyler. "Your turn comes later. Maybe."

"I get everyone's approval by being a terrific person."

"But how do you *do* that?"

"I…I find out what people want, what they expect me to be, then I become that. Or give them that."

"What if they all expect different things?"

"…It gets harder."

"And of course it eventually becomes impossible, because there's not enough of you to go around. Then what do you do?"

"I try even harder."

"And if that doesn't work?"

"I become depressed and brood about it."

"Good," said Tyler. He sometimes seems delighted by my various misfortunes.

"That's good?" I said.

"No, I mean it's good that you understand the impossibility of getting everyone's approval. So what's the solution?"

"Don't get caught in big crowds where there are lots of people who all may have different expectations of me."

"No."

"Limit my social circle to only those people who have the same expectations of me."

"No again."

"Is there a web site?" I said. "Something like www. approval.com?"

"There's a line in the Book that says, *Some of us sought out sordid places, hoping to find understanding, companionship and approval.* The question is, Why sordid places to find approval?"

"…Because…that's where I belong?"

"Maybe. Say more."

"Because…in those kind of places nobody expects anything of me."

"Right," said Tyler. "The bar is set so low, everybody gets over it. And nobody's going to say, *You'd be better off if you were driving a Beamer instead of that domestic pile of junk.* Or, *That tie doesn't really go with that suit.* There are *no* expectations. You are…what?"

"…Approved of?…Accepted? Okay?"

"All of the above. There you will indeed find understanding, companionship and approval. You have common enemies …Anyone with a job. The *po*-lice. People who are living Uptown. All those who are Better Off. The list is long."

"Is that why I spent all that time in those crummy joints?"

"Probably," he said. "They all think you're okay because you're just like they are. You have their absolute approval, which you desperately need because…because?"

"Is that a question?"

"Yes."

"I need their approval because…I feel better when people approve of me."

"Partially correct," said Tyler. "Dig a little deeper."

"I need their approval because…my life is in the tank if I don't get it."

"Didn't we agree at one time that life was an inside job?"

"I don't remember." I said.

"Let me remember for you. We did. And if life works from the inside out, if it's an inside job, then why do we need someone else's approval?"

"Because…I don't really believe that life works from the inside out, and I don't know how to approve of myself?"

"For some reason many of us believe that self-disapproval is a virtue. Here's what some wise spiritual soul had to say about it…

When you believe self-disapproval is a virtue, and you believe in virtue, then you obviously find yourself in a position where the more you disapprove of yourself, the better person you think you are—a contradiction of the most insidious nature..."

"Seth?"

"I think so," he said. "So what's the guilt about?"

"What guilt?"

"The guilt that keeps you from approving of yourself."

"I grew up guilty," I said.

"Why?"

"...I don't know why, Maestro. But I suspect that you were the same way. Why did *you* grow up guilty?"

"Early on, when I was young and somewhat innocent, I was given some bogus information."

"And who was it that gave you this...misinformation?

"The Big People. The gods and goddesses who directed and controlled my life: parents, teachers, coaches, priests, all those in positions of power. They were the people who were supposed to teach me things that would help me."

"And what did they teach you?" I said.

"They taught me that the world was a very dangerous place, and that I should proceed on my journey with extreme caution. They taught me The Rules, having to do with being obedient, not coveting my neighbor's new bike, and loving my mother and father, who were God's representatives here on earth. They told me that if I tried a little harder, I'd be a little better, though no matter how hard I tried, I would never be better enough."

"I remember the hymn, O Lord I Am Not Worthy."

"Precisely...They taught me to be dissatisfied with who I was and what I was, that I was a person badly in need of something called salvation. All of which sounded okay except I had trouble with the loving part when my father was using my mother as a punching bag while she was pleading for divine assistance. Then I began to wonder about this God who was sending these representatives to take care of me. And when I became old enough, I got to be used as a punching bag, too. Evidently there're some age restrictions involved."

"You have to be a certain age so you can be a responsible punching bag."

"Then," said Tyler, "the priest said I had to do penance for something that happened in the Garden of Eden a long time ago having to do with the first dysfunctional family. Implying, of course, that I was guilty of something."

"You ever figure out what it was?"

"…They called it Original Sin, but I could never figure out my part in it. You know, what we look for in the fourth column of the Fourth Step Inventory: *What was my part in it?* Never could get a good grip on it."

"Check out the Baltimore Catechism. It's all in there."

"What would I do without you, Edward?"

"You'd be completely lost, Maestro. Believe me."

"And your guilt, Edward? Why do you think you're unable to find favor with yourself? Why do you need all that approval coming from external sources?"

"I got the Original Sin treatment, too, but it didn't mean much because I couldn't identify with any of it. It was too abstract, too…distant. What really got my attention was the life-size crucifix that Brother Rupert hauled into class one day when I was in the third grade. This thing was huge. He went on and on about the wounds, and the blood, and the pain, and topped it off with the declaration that we evil third-graders, were responsible for pounding those nails into the hands and feet of gentle Jesus. I was in tears."

"You were probably unaware," said Tyler, "of just how evil third-graders could be."

"Well, I knew Marvin Schmidt was evil because every day he came to school he punched me on the arm as hard as he could. But I didn't know about the rest. For a while I was terrified that my mother and father were going to find out what I had done."

"Did they?"

"...I don't know. They never said."

"You know," said Tyler, "the word guilt is not used in the first hundred and sixty-four pages of the Big Book, and guilty is only mentioned once. That's the story about the man who ruined his business rival by lying about a sum of money he had received. If he copped to it, he was afraid it would ruin his partner and destroy his own livelihood. But, as the story goes, he decided it was better to risk it than to stand before his Creator guilty of such ruinous behavior."

"So he fessed up?"

"He did."

"And what happened?"

"The Book tells us that his action met with widespread approval, and he became one of the most trusted citizens in his town."

"Hurray for the Ninth Step."

"Indeed," he said. "But, lest we digress too far, tell me what all this means."

"It means that...we need lots of outside approval because most of us grew up without a healthy sense of self and find it extremely difficult to approve of ourselves. It's like that thing you always say...You can't hate yourself and love God."

"And where do we get this approval from?"

"Initially, from the Community, Maestro. You remember the old saying ...We'll love you till you can love yourself."

"I do remember. Though I also remember that it was not popular with the Olde Tymers. They thought it reeked of New Age sentimentality."

"But we can forgive them, right?"

"No forgiveness necessary," said Tyler.

"Because they were afraid that any deviation from what they considered The Word was dangerous."

"True. They were zealous about guarding the program from any hint of error. But who could blame them? In the beginning, nobody knew if this thing would really work, if it would stand the test of time. But we've evolved and changed."

"You think we'll continue to change?" I said.

"I do. Bill W and some of his cronies were conducting seances in the beginning. LSD has been mentioned. But I think that as long as the foundation is firm, meaning the Twelve Steps, I don't think we need fear change or experiments in other spiritual realms."

"Wait till the God Squad gets hold of you."

"I've always loved the part in the Twelve and Twelve that says something to the effect that...*No AA can compel another to do anything; nobody can be punished or expelled.*"

"I think you've said that before."

"It's worth repeating" he said. "So...We clear on this week's lesson?"

"We are," I said. "Let it be known that henceforth Edward Bear will honor himself and his interior connection to a Higher Power, will trust the Process as it unfolds in his life, being aware at all times that the Universe inclines toward him and wishes him well."

"Just remember that no matter how long you've been sober, being an alcoholic, being an addict of any kind, means you're always at risk. Always."

"No safe harbor? No place of rest and ease?"

"No. You will always be standing next to the abyss, inches from the edge. Complacency kills. As the saying goes, *If eternal vigilance is the price of freedom, what's the price of sobriety?*"

"Same deal, eh?" I said.

"Eternal vigilance indeed. So next week we'll tackle the Second Great Fallacy...*If I can't figure out how it can happen, it can't happen.*"

"That's a fallacy?...Just kidding, Maestro."

"I'd like you to explain what that means."

"How come I have to explain *your* Great Fallacies? I keep thinking that should be your job."

"It's your job because you relapsed."

"So I get all the crap because I slipped."

"You didn't slip, Edward. Slipped sounds like something accidental. Relapsed is the proper word."

"Damn it, Tyler, I don't..."

"The anger is understandable, Edward. Just realize who you should be angry with."

That man can be impossible sometimes.

CHAPTER FOUR

*If, in the last few years, you haven't discarded
a major opinion or acquired a new one, check
your pulse. You may be dead.*
                    Gelett Burgess

"I had a dream about you, Maestro. Just last night."

"Something exciting, I hope. Like me and Dorothy
Lamour."

"...Who's Dorothy Lamour?"

"Never mind," said Tyler.

"It was you and Mercedes and you were brewing this
awful concoction in a big kettle—something with maybe the
eye of a newt and the skin of a virgin frog in it. And were
trying to convince me that I ought to drink it."

"You think it was poison?" said Tyler.

"The thought crossed my mind."

"What did it taste like?"

"You kiddin'? You think I drank it?"

"Could have been something pleasant, maybe liquid
Viagra."

"Why would you give me liquid Viagra?" I said.

"Why would I try to poison you?"

"You're doing that answering a question with a question
thing again."

"Sorry…How did the dream end?"

"Just before I woke up, I had a vision of what would happen if I *did* drink it."

"And what was that?" said Tyler

"Well, after I drank it, my head began to swell until it was about ten times the size of my body. It was so big I toppled over and couldn't get my head off the floor."

"Interesting, Edward. What do you make of it?"

"Here I had this huge head and this little tiny body."

"So…what do you…"

"I was at the mercy of this gigantic head, which really couldn't do anything because my body was so small it couldn't control anything."

"Keep going," said Tyler. "You may be on to something."

"…There's no place to go, Maestro. I'm just stuck there with my head on the floor, a body and neck so small it can't lift it. I'm just…there. Helpless."

"Powerless?"

"…You could say that." I could tell by the tone of his voice that he was getting ready to attack.

"So we could say that a big head, a head full of ideas and even wisdom, is not always an asset. I mean if it gets too big."

"…We could say that…With some reservations."

"And what might they be, the reservations?"

"Well…if your head was actually too big, I mean so big it made even walking around impossible, then…that could be a real problem. Maybe with no reservations. But if your head was just a little too big…"

"Semi-large?"

"Yeah," I said. "Semi-large might be okay."

"Like semi, as in truck."

"Sort of…" I have to be careful here; it's places like this that he tries to trip me up with his oh-so-innocent questions. "If it was semi-large you could at least get around, think about things, maybe even figure out a few things."

"Might be able to think things through, make some decisions…you know, based on prior experience. Which you had catalogued in your semi-large head for just such occasions."

"What are you trying to get me to say, Tyler?"

"I'm not trying to get you to say anything, Edward. That would be highly manipulative, and of course I wouldn't do that."

"Ho ho ho."

"But I *was* going to suggest that the dream might have been trying to tell you that if your head gets too full of ideas, that instead of working to your advantage, it might actually be a handicap. Maybe there'd be no room for other things. Like miracles."

"You think my head's too big?" I said.

"It was your dream, Edward. My suspicion is that *you* think your head's too big, that you would be better off with fewer facts or ideas and more trust."

"I don't think that at all. Actually I think the more ideas you have the better off you are. Trust is for people who are short of ideas."

"You might take note of the fact that your very best thinking, your very best ideas concerning life, got you into recovery. You know, like, *Some of us tried to hold on to our old ideas and the result was nil,* et cetera…"

"My thinking was okay, it was my judgment that was off."

"Not likely," said Tyler.

"You think it was significant that I had this dream the night before we were going to meet and discuss the Second Great Fallacy?"

"It does seem to relate, doesn't it? *If I can't figure out how it can happen, it can't happen.* No room for miracles?"

"…As you know, I have some reservations about the miracle stuff…But didn't this Higher Power, whatever It is, give us brains so we could do just that—figure things out."

"You ever try to figure out where your thoughts come from?" said Tyler. "Ever try to follow them to their source?"

"Don't start that stuff again."

"There's nothing wrong with brains," he said. "Or intelligence. But because we live in a three-dimensional world, when we try to apply three-dimensional thinking to four – or five-dimensional spiritual issues, we get into trouble. The same rules don't apply."

"Did I nod off and miss something? We just get a couple of extra dimensions from somewhere?"

I love it when Tyler gets that look on his face, like he's groping for the right words to clarify a statement he just made that doesn't make a lick of sense. Even to him.

"Let me give you an example," he said.

"Why don't you do that, Maestro. At this point I definitely think we need some clarity."

"Would you agree that we live in a three-dimensional world?"

"For the sake of this discussion, I'll agree with that."

"Example A…One day I was thinking about some amends that I figure I'd never be able to make. They were to the guys on the ammunition ship I was aboard during the Korean War. Get it? I couldn't figure out how it could happen? So…"

"This isn't another war story, is it Boss?"

"This is about the Second Great Fallacy, Edward...*If I can't figure out how it can happen, it can't happen.* So... some of my...potential amends were pretty heavy duty. Unsavory, you could say. I came out of a blackout once and was pounding my best friend's head against the steel bulkhead."

"...Your best *friend*?"

"Edward...Please. Just listen."

"Roger."

"So one day an e-mail arrives inviting me to the First Annual Reunion of the U.S.S. Chara, being held right here in our town. The First Annual Reunion, Edward. How did they get my e-mail address? I haven't heard from anyone on that ship in fifty years. Why, after all that time, do I get an invite to the Reunion? Why is it here in Our Town?"

"A fabulous mystery, Boss. But, as I recall, you always warned me about getting too involved with all those W words, like Why, When, Where, and Who."

"Jesus..." said Tyler. "So naturally I go and there are all these guys I was on the ship with. So I make my amends, though most of them don't have a clue what I'm talking about."

"How about coincidence, Maestro?"

"What's the Fallacy?"

"...*If I can't figure out how it can happen, it can't happen.*"

"The Reunion fall into that category?"

"...Maybe, but..."

"You have to stretch the imagination a long way to come up with a scenario like that."

"I'm not convinced," I said. "And I certainly don't see a Miracle Hand in all this."

"Here's another one. I fly into New York a couple of years ago and call Central Office about five o'clock in the afternoon to try and find a meeting. What do I get? An answering machine. So I'm fuming about here we are in one of the world's biggest cities and they don't have anyone at Central Office after five o'clock. I can't figure out how I'm going to get a meeting directory. Get it? I can't figure out how I'm..."

" I sense a miracle on the horizon."

"So, the next morning I'm walking down Broadway near Times Square and here comes a guy from my home group.

From my home group, Edward. In the middle of New York City. Right away I launch into my resentment about not being able to go to a meeting because Central Office didn't have anyone manning the phones after five and I couldn't get a meeting directory. He reaches into his coat, pulls out a directory and hands it to me."

"I'll take Door Number Three, the one labeled Coincidence."

"Edward, there are maybe fifteen million people in New York City. What are the odds of me running into somebody from my home group who just happens to have a meeting directory in his pocket?"

"Evidently a lot better than you thought," I said.

"No, it's the fact that we're all somehow connected through a Higher Power."

"Perhaps with New Age Golden Thread, Boss?"

"I don't know how to describe it. What I do know is that if I'm working my side of the street to the best of my ability, carrying the message, doing my deal, the right people show up when needed, ready and willing to lend a hand."

"You really believe that?"

"I do," said Tyler. "It's one of those experiences I have catalogued in my semi-large head."

"And you *don't* believe in mistakes."

"No," he said.

"So you don't think it was a mistake that I drank again…I mean after twelve years in recovery."

"No. I don't believe it was a mistake."

"Then what was it?" I said. "Some kind of cryptic message from the Great Pumpkin?"

"It's called a Lesson, Edward, as are all the things we experience."

"Some lesson. All things considered, I'd just as soon have had the lesson come in some other way."

"In all probability there were mini-lessons that came before the relapse-lesson, trial balloons, so to speak. But they didn't get your attention. Perhaps a minor resentment was ignored until it became a major resentment."

"You think I drank over a resentment?" I said.

"Since, as the Big Book tells us, resentment is the number one offender, destroying, note the word, Edward… *destroying* more alcoholics than anything else, it's possible that a smoldering resentment may have caught fire and had something to do with your relapse."

"You think I'm resentful of Samantha, don't you?"

"You get to pick your own resentments, Edward."

"Just because she stepped out on me…with that obnoxious son of a bitch, Frank. God…"

"Only you're not too sure it was Frank, are you? Or anybody."

"I'm almost a hundred percent positive."

"I don't want to belabor the issue," he said, "but the Big Book says it best…

...but with the alcoholic, this business of resentment is infinitely grave. We found that it is fatal. For when harboring...another key word here, Edward...when harboring such feelings we cut ourselves off from the sunlight of the spirit. The insanity of alcohol returns and we drink again...

"Notice that it doesn't say we drink again and then the insanity returns. It says the insanity returns first, and then we drink."

"Let's get back to the Second Great Fallacy," I said. I didn't want to get him started on resentments; we'd be here all night. "I'm still favoring the coincidence theory."

"That's not the point," said Tyler.

"...No?"

"No. The point is that since *I* couldn't figure out how it was going to happen, I assumed that it couldn't possibly happen, thereby limiting The Force. Or the Great Pumpkin. Or God even...Which is the height of intellectual arrogance. But the signs, Noble Student, the signs are everywhere."

"You've said that before—*The signs are everywhere. We just can't see them.* What does that mean?"

"Basically," he said, "you see the signs you expect to see. The rest get filtered out. Like the opportunity signs. Or the danger signs. And the emotional and spiritual riches that lie hidden in plain sight."

"Why?"

"Why do we ignore the signs?" said Tyler. "Haven't we been over this before?"

"Probably. But I keep forgetting."

"The simplest thing I can say is that we've been taught that they don't exist. It's like you have blinders on. Or a severe case of tunnel vision. You don't see God because you don't believe in God."

"And I suppose you do...see God."

"Let's leave that for later discussion. In the meantime, read the preface to Leaves of Grass."

"Whitman?"

"Yes...Now tell me some of the things you think *can't* happen."

"Lots of things..."

"For instance."

"I'll never have a decent, long-term relationship. I'm doomed to have annual unions that turn into marriages that don't usually last very long. It's pitiful. Another one is that I'll never get published on my own. I'll be playing Boswell to your Johnson forever. If I ever do manage to get published it will be at a minor house with no advertising budget that will go out of business shortly after publishing my novel."

"Those are both false," said Tyler.

"Easy for you to say. You've had a long-term relationship. Maybe more than one. Even your Vampire friend probably counts. And people think that you actually write these books, forgetting how much effort I put into them."

"Let me explain. What really happens when you believe something *can't* happen, is that you simply limit The Force, which needs your cooperation to be fully effective. This is a joint venture, Noble Student, you and your Higher Power. But It needs your cooperation, your trust, your belief."

"It hasn't proved worthy of my trust yet."

"Wrong sequence," said Tyler. "Remember the waving statue. You have to trust *It* first. Then your attitude and your outlook and your belief will allow certain...events, certain experiences to come into your life. Dream big, Edward."

"Tyler…"

"You see, you're handicapped with some of the same basic attitudes that I had. And still have to some extent."

"Like what?" I said.

"A little too much fondness for my limited intellectual capacity. It's called arrogance."

"You think I'm arrogant?"

"I'm not saying that."

"You're…implying that."

"No. Let me work it from my side of the street… *My* arrogance tells me that if I can't figure out how it can happen, it can't happen. Simple enough, but it also reduces my intellectual life to the complexity of a Dodge Ball game and takes all the magic out of it."

"Ah…"

"Ah, what?"

"I don't get it, don't like it…"

"Remember that once a mental map is formed, it conditions all your perceptions. It's the filter through which you view life."

"And the mental map is formed by?"

"By the Committee," said Tyler. "By the Voices in your head, placed there by all those charged with your education and welfare. Parents. Teachers. Peers. The Vultures and the Doves. The Angels and the Demons."

"Now you're saying I've got a bad map?"

"You do. You're viewing life through a splintered lens."

"So how do I fix the…"

"The Steps, of course," he said.

"Of course…That's your answer to everything."

"Not everything, but it's a good starting point. But lest the evening go on too long, let's end with a quote from Emerson ...*People only see what they are prepared to see.*"

"Okay, okay. I surrender," I said. "You're giving me a nosebleed. What's for next week?"

"Maybe we'll try the First Great Discovery."

"*My way doesn't work?*"

"That's it."

"...I want you to know that I'm really working on this stuff, Maestro. Busting my buns. Sometimes I don't think you appreciate that."

"Oh, but I do, Edward. You don't know how much you're helping me."

"...Really?"

"Really. When I'm talking to you or listening to you, I'm not thinking about myself. And when I'm not thinking about myself, I'm automatically healing. That's how it works."

"I should maybe charge you for healing services," I said.

"Don't get carried away, Edward."

CHAPTER FIVE

Life is God's novel. Let him write it.
Isaac Bashevis Singer

"So Maestro, how did you make all these discoveries we're going to be discussing?"

"Mercedes and I had sex last night," said Tyler.

Just when I think I've heard it all, he comes up with something like this.

"So you must be on speaking terms again. But what does that mean? Having sex."

"Just a comment," said Tyler. "Information, if you will. I thought you might be interested."

"What made you think that?"

"You always seem interested in what we do. So I thought the fact that we had sex might interest you."

"What kind of sex might that have been, Maestro?"

"…Consensual."

"I know it was consensual," I said. "I didn't expect you to attack her."

"A little missionary, a little swaperoo."

"A little swaperoo," I said. "That's a new term?"

"No. Old. Very old. Before your time."

"And how old is Mercedes?"

"She could be sixty. Could even be seventy or eighty."

"And you're in your seventies."

"Seventy-two," he said. "Remember that movie, Harold and Maude?"

"Never mind the movie. God, I don't believe you guys. What do you do, lick each other."

"You were watching?"

I had to get him off the subject.

"I don't want to talk about this anymore, Tyler. I want to talk about the Five Great Discoveries. Starting with number one."

"I discovered another one last night. That makes six."

"Tyler, I don't want to talk about you and Mercedes. I don't even want to think about the elderly rattling around in bed together. Especially you and Mercedes. I find the image very unwholesome."

"I used to think that, too."

"What changed your mind?"

"Getting old," he said.

"Is Mercedes married?"

"I don't think so."

"You don't know?"

"I never asked. It didn't seem important."

"God..." I just shook my head. "You may end up with a long amends list."

"And a long gratitude list to go with it."

"My mentor, my hero, out having his way with elderly women. You're impossible, Maestro."

"Thank you. We should all try to be impossible and unpredictable as we age. Laugh more, cry less; there is already an abundance of sadness in the world. Carry the message: Life is possible without alcohol and its companion drugs. Even without gambling away the rent money, or eating chocolate cake for breakfast, or engaging in degrading sexual activities, or…"

"Let's get on with the First Discovery."

"If you insist."

"*My way doesn't work*," I said, hoping to get him headed in the right direction.

"Right. Never has, probably never will. I often wonder why it took me so long to come to that simple conclusion. And let's tie it in with the Second Discovery: *God has in store for me much better things than I have in store for me.*"

"The next obvious question, Maestro, is why?"

"Precisely. Why doesn't my way work? Good question. Other people have *ways* that work. Some people have it all figured out by the time they're nine or ten years old…*I want to be a doctor. I want to be a pilot…I want to be an alcoholic?* That sound right? Anybody you know start out that way?"

"Can't think of anybody off hand…Maybe Uncle Frank."

"Let's say nobody."

"Okay," I said.

"So what was the *way* that didn't work for us?"

"I'll bite. What *was* it?"

"My way," said Tyler, like it should be obvious.

"I know that, Maestro. But what was it about your way or my way that didn't work?"

"Precisely because it was my way, it was doomed to failure. My way accepted no advice, ignored direction, shunned all suggestions…My way says, *Oh, I've done that and it doesn't work*, whether I've actually done it or not. Your essential quick study. *I hate oysters…Ever eat one?…Well, no, but I hate oysters anyway…*it's the essence of what Herbert Spencer called, *Contempt prior to investigation.* My razor sharp mind leaps ahead of the conversation, makes microsecond decisions based on faulty, or no, information and comes to conclusions that only a lunatic would accept. All done with a straight face."

"Your encyclopedic knowledge of trivia and your sparkling vocabulary carry the day and people are awed by the fact that you have such a grasp of the situation...When actually you don't know shit."

"And am not about to learn anything either," he said, "because I already know everything. At least everything worthwhile. Everything important. That's my way. Bluff your way through life. Use the Steamroller technique when subtlety fails. Develop a really large vocabulary and crush the opposition. Justify your actions at all cost."

"How did you discover that your way didn't work?"

"The first inklings came when I found myself locked up in the Old County Jail in L.A. in the spring of 1965. Malcolm X had just been assassinated, the Watts Riots were several months away, and yours truly was seated on the concrete floor awaiting trial."

"That got your attention?" I said.

"That was the beginning. I was thirty-one years old, married, two kids, unemployable by any standard. My way, my unique and daring way of approaching life had culminated in having my skinny ass planted on the stone cold floor of the Old County Jail. Remember James Cagney—*Top of the world, Ma?*"

"White Heat?" I suggested.

"...That was me...The point being that it finally occurred to me that the things I had been doing had never worked and probably never would. I was a construction worker, Edward. A hod carrier, a ditch digger, an unloader of freight cars, a day laborer. I, who was going to be the first dishwasher to read and fully understand Finnegan's Wake, had come a cropper during an armed robbery and was looking at a five-to-life sentence."

"Heavy."

"Heavy indeed. But as disastrous as it was, there was not yet an overwhelming *Ah ha!* a real awareness that my path, my way, as arduous and treacherous as it was, was perhaps not the only one possible."

"So, even with the consequences of your behavior staring you in the face, you still thought that your way might work."

"I did," said Tyler. "I thought maybe, just maybe, I had overlooked something. I wondered what had gone wrong. Not what had *I* done wrong, but simply what had *gone* wrong. What mysterious aspect of the gods had entered my life at just the wrong time to make me a victim one-more-time? The idea that alcohol played a large part in my misfortunes didn't enter my mind. My guess is that, to some degree, you had the same thought process."

"I...sometimes entertained similar thoughts."

"It's time for a little Truth Telling, Edward. Truth is, you probably thought that since you were always right, everyone else had to be wrong..."

"Well, I..."

"You may have suffered from a serious case of terminal uniqueness. It's not uncommon. Jails are full of people who had answers to questions that no one ever asked, who had lots of information but no way to connect the dots. And I personally did consider the possibility that there might be other ways that worked, but only for the poor, misguided Others, the Rabble, the Great Unwashed. But not for Mister Unique. I said what I always said..."

"And what was that?"

"...My comeback was always, *You don't understand.* Oh, that might work for *you*, but I'm different. I'm special. I'm too sensitive. Besides being Mister Unique, I'm Mister Sensitive ...I'm a Poet living among the Philistines, unappreciated, unloved and, above all, misunderstood."

"So what do you do," I said, "when you suddenly realize that *Your way doesn't work,* that thirty-one years of putting one foot in front of the other has only earned you a seat on the concrete floor of the Old County Jail."

"First you try not to think about it because it's too depressing, then you feel very sorry for yourself and wallow in self-pity for a while. Then, if you're very lucky, it may occur to you that *Your way doesn't work* because maybe you're not as smart as you thought you were and *Your Way* always included large amounts of alcohol and at least a few of its companion drugs."

"Man, I did the same thing. Not the prison deal, but a relationship that finally drove me to my knees and forced me to consider, for the first time, that something might be amiss in my approach to life."

"Hence, hitting bottom and realizing that *My way doesn't work,*" he said.

"But how do we know that somebody else's way *does* work?"

"We don't. All you have to know is that your way *doesn't* work. With that knowledge comes the gift of desperation. Who was it that said, *Life begins on the other side of despair?*"

"...Sartre?"

"Maybe...And who said, *Life is a series of surrenders?*"

"You did," I said.

65

"And I probably stole it from somebody else. What does the Big Book say about surrender?"

"...Surrender is the answer to all my problems?"

"That's *acceptance* is the answer to all my problems. From Doctor Paul's story. And actually the Big Book doesn't even mention surrender in the first hundred and sixty-four pages."

"Then how come we talk about surrender all the time?"

"That leads us into the Second Great Discovery... *God has in store for me much better things than I have in store for me*."

"Meaning?"

"If my way doesn't work, First Discovery, and if God has in store for me much better things than I have in store for me, why not turn it over to Him and let Him run the show?"

"Surrender, in other words."

"Surrender. Third Step, Second Discovery. Surrender is defined as being willing to—*relinquish possession or control, to give up or abandon*...your way. Which, of course, doesn't work anyway."

"Without really knowing if this Power, this Force is going to do any better than you did. Or do anything."

"Right," said Tyler. "The despair must be total, as must the willingness to try anything...And to endure anything."

"I was even willing to try Alcoholics Anonymous and your crummy three-drums-and-a-whistle spiritual marching band."

"You were willing," said Tyler "...for a while. Then something happened."

"I was willing for a long time, Maestro. Twelve years is a considerable amount of time."

"Granted. But then something happened. Did you withdraw the decision you made in the Third Step…to turn your will and your life over to the care of God? Third Step can be a deal-breaker. What lie did you tell yourself before you picked up a drink? Was the night so dark and frightening that the only thing that would chase away the demons was a drink?"

"In truth, I think I said to myself that thing you always call the Fatal Phrase."

"…What's the use?"

"That's the one," I said.

"And instead of calling someone, taking some kind of action, you simply had a drink, thinking…what? That you could just have one and not tell anyone? That you could take a vacation from recovery and come back any time you wanted to? You know better than that. How many times have you seen people walk out the door and never come back? Or come back on a slab. Or in handcuffs."

"What I remember was that I hated my life. I remember thinking, *If this is as good as it gets, why bother*? There was one more relationship down the drain. One more attempt and one more failure. I get up every morning, go to a meeting, talk to some people, go to a dead-end job, then come home, open up a can of Dinty Moore Beef Stew, watch Desperate Housewives and go to bed. This is a life? I was spared an alcoholic death to do this?"

"Primary purpose," said Tyler.

"Oh…primary purpose my ass."

"Stay sober and carry the message," he said.

"Great. Well, I've got a message for everyone…I don't want to carry *the* message, *a* message, *your* message, or *anybody's* message."

"We are driven by a hundred forms of fear, self-delusion, self-seeking and self-pity…"

"Will you stop quoting the Big Book. I know what it says …I've committed large portions of it to memory, but…"

"But what?" said Tyler.

"…But I can't *do* it, Tyler. I *know* the words, but they're just words. They don't *mean* anything anymore."

"Who do you dislike most?" he said.

"…Besides you?"

"Yeah."

"Me."

"Why?"

"I can't help it."

"So now you're a victim," said Tyler.

"…It's a good thing there aren't any weapons in the house."

"I'd be dead?"

"Most likely."

"For what? For telling the truth? For pointing out that you hate yourself because you're not perfect? That you continue to punish yourself for real or imagined faults?"

"Oh, Tyler…"

"I've always cherished the fact that Bill W, who I consider a true visionary, was something less than the saint people wanted to make him."

"How so?" I said.

"It's no secret that Bill was something of a philanderer, a notion that doesn't get much play around the rooms because everybody wants to think of him as a saint who went to the mountain one night and came down with the Twelve Steps."

"…I've heard that."

"I believe this Higher Power, God if you will, picked Bill and Dr. Bob to carry this life-affirming message of surrender and service because they were less than perfect. You remember they had just six steps for the first couple of years."

"The word-of-mouth program."

"Right. Then one night, in the space of thirty minutes, Bill stretched the six steps into twelve. In the Grapevine article he says, *Uninspired as I felt...I set down certain principles which ...turned out to be twelve in number.*"

"No stone tablets from the mountain."

"No," said Tyler. "And no people in robes, no incense, no candles, no purification rituals. And no intermediaries. The Great Pumpkin picked a couple of drunks to pass along the message that people could get sober and stay sober."

"Love and tolerance..."

"I love the fact that Bill, when he was just a few weeks from dying, asked for three shots of whiskey. Of course they didn't give him any. But a couple of days later he asked for four shots."

"Though he didn't get the first three, the next time he asked for four. A typical drunk right to the end, eh?"

"How can you not love a guy like that? It gives us all a chance. It means you don't have to be perfect to get sober. You just have to be willing...Which means, Noble Student, that you can get off your own case and trust your Higher Power."

"You're suggesting a surrender of sorts, a plan where I stop being so self-obsessed and self-critical."

"You have a mandate," said Tyler. "You have a unique opportunity to be of service. You can help where others can't, as it says in the Big Book. Bill and Bob discovered the secret early on—the key that unlocked the door was the willingness to be of service. You can't will yourself to believe in God. That may or may not happen for you. But you can take an action …which we're going to talk about next week."

"You think I drank because I wasn't into action?"

"Doesn't make any difference what I think," said Tyler. "You're the only one who knows the answer to that…But perhaps you were resting on your laurels."

"…Maybe."

"Maybe you looked in the mirror one day and thought, Hey, look at me. Ain't I somethin'? I'm a dozen years sober. I've written books about recovery. I know lots. I'm bulletproof. Maybe the rules don't apply anymore."

"I don't think I actually went that far," I said.

"We're as sick as we are secretive."

"Stop already."

"Somewhere in your program," said Tyler, "you expected a reward for twelve years of sobriety, maybe a wonderful relationship, a book contract, some special gift from your Higher Power as an acknowledgement of your dozen years of dedicated service."

"I didn't expect anything."

"But you did, Edward, and when you didn't get it you employed the fatal phrase, *What's the use*. Originally we say, *All I want is to be sober*, but after a while that's not enough. Then we want things, and goodies, and cars and jobs and houses and respect and mooooooore. It's a disease of more. Then we are afflicted with the *If onlys* and the *What ifs*. *If only I had a better job…If only Mary Lou would go out with me*. Gimme, gimme, gimme…Come to the Ca-ba-ret."

I hate it when he starts singing.

"Okay, okay," I said. "I am driven by your ruthless attack on my character, to admit that sometimes, if only rarely, I entertained the idea that my life would be better, maybe a lot better, if I had some of those things."

"You willing to let the Great Pumpkin work in your life?"

"I…think so."

"You think so?" said Tyler. "After all this you just think so?"

"Okay, I'm willing."

"Even if it means losing your job and never having a decent relationship? Even if all you get is just sobriety? Nothing else?"

"…Yes," I said.

"Because that's all you get promised—sobriety. The rest is gravy and not everybody gets the gravy. Some people get sober and lose jobs, get divorced, lose children, get incurable diseases…and continue to stay sober and carry the message. Primary purpose, Edward. That's the one and only reason you're sober."

"I have seen the enemy, and it is me?"

"Indeed. So relax, Noble Student. Someone, Who has your best interests at heart, is minding the store. Your job is to…?"

"Suit up and show up and carry the message?"

"Right. And get out of the results business. Next week: *Action is the magic word*."

CHAPTER SIX

There is action and more action
Alcoholics Anonymous

"And the Third Great Discovery, Edward?"

"*Action is the magic word.*"

"Good," said Tyler. "What does it mean?"

"It's…self-explanatory," I said. "*Action is the magic word.* You might just as well ask me what magic means?"

"Okay…What does magic mean?"

"Not literally, Maestro. Magic is…like magic. Slight of hand. Prestidigitation."

"Nice word," he said dryly.

"Thanks."

"You're dancing, Edward. Tripping around the edges of ideas and definitions. Skimming the surface when perhaps you should be delving a little deeper."

"Well, if the questions had more…substance, Maestro, I might have better luck with the answers."

"You want something meaty like…What's the meaning of life?"

"Too meaty," I said

"So define action."

"Action is…doing something."

"Is thinking an action?"

"…Can be."

"When is it not an action?"

"Jesus, Tyler, what are you trying to get at?"

"Since action is the magic word, and the Big Book tells us there is *action and more action,* I'm curious about what your definition of action is."

"Did you and Mercedes have sex last night?"

"I thought you weren't interested in that," said Tyler.

"Given the choice I am more interested in that than I am in trying to define action."

"Try anyway…Does action have to cause change to truly be defined as action?"

"…Yes and no."

"Not acceptable."

"…Sometimes."

"Also not acceptable. Action is mentioned twenty-five times in the first hundred and sixty-four pages."

"And of course you've counted them," I said.

"…Indicating its importance."

"And also indicating the shallowness of your life. You and Mercedes ought to get together and plan something exciting, like a wheelchair race. Or maybe just a heavy breathing contest. Something that wouldn't be too taxing."

"What's the opposite of action, Edward?"

"…You're just not going to let it go, are you?

"The short answer is no…What determines if an action is good?"

"…The result?"

"Is letting go of old ideas a good action?" said Tyler.

"Since most of my old ideas led directly or indirectly into recovery, I'd have to call letting go of old ideas a good action."

"Is surrender an action?" he said.

"As you always say, *Surrender is a very active process.*"

"You mean I don't just turn in my sword?"

"Negative, Maestro. Remember Step Three."

"So how do we manage to experience this thing called a spiritual awakening?"

"We...take action," I said.

"What action?"

"The Steps, of course...*Having had a spiritual awakening as the* result *of these steps, we tried to carry this message*... et cetera."

"So it seems," said Tyler, "that we are going to have to participate in our own recovery. If you expect to just sit in those meetings and absorb recovery, you're going to wait a long time."

"It's the zero sum game you always talk about."

"The equation is perfect. No action equals no action. We can turn to the Bhagavad Gita for clarification about action."

"Tyler...Nobody reads the Gita anymore. Get with it. Update your portfolio. That was a fad during the fifties and sixties when the Beatles were doing all that Maharishi stuff. People are reading Ken Wilber, David Bohm, and Rupert Sheldrake now. You're still stuck with Gurdjieff and P.D. Ouspensky. Ancient history."

Ignoring my comments, as he usually does, Tyler moved on without missing a beat.

"You know the story..."

Again demonstrating one of his most annoying habits, assuming that I do know and then proceeding without waiting for a reply.

"...Krishna, who is actually an incarnation of God in the guise of a charioteer, is having this conversation with

Arjuna, who represents Everyman. You can think of it as a conversation between a cab driver who is maybe Thomas Merton and a passenger who is Keith Richards...."

"Keith Richards?"

"Well, maybe not Keith Richards. How about Dr. Phil?"

"Closer, but..."

"Anyway, you get the picture."

Of course, he doesn't care if I get the picture or not. He just wants to make his point.

"The point is, (see, I told you) that the Gita informs us that *action is better than inaction*, reaffirming our position three thousand years before the Big Book was written. Plus, it says that it is not material possessions that are the problem, but our selfish attachment to them."

"Right out of the Big Book," I said. "*Selfishness, self-centeredness! That, we think, is the root of our troubles.*"

"Krishna instructs Arjuna in the path of liberation through action without attachment...As in *Get out of the results business.* Do you believe that all actions make a difference?"

"...A difference in what?"

"A difference in the world."

"I'm not getting this clearly. What kind of a difference are we talking about?"

"A difference in how things happen in the world," he said. "It's been said that everything we say, do, or think makes a difference."

"Maybe I could make a difference in Pretty Sarah's life. Perhaps if I concentrated, I could influence how she feels about going out with me."

"Sarah, at the Friday Night meeting who is new to recovery?" said Tyler.

"Hey, I'm a newcomer, too."

75

"Which makes it even worse."

"We go over this every time I find a new woman to date."

"No, not every time. Just those times when the new love interest happens to be new to recovery."

"Well, Maestro, somebody's going to ask her out. Some creep who doesn't have her best interest at heart."

"Like you do."

"Exactly. Just think of all those slugs at the Friday Night Meeting, ready to pounce on any new woman brave enough to enter."

"So better you than them?"

"Of course. I'll at least insist she get a sponsor, a woman sponsor, and do the Steps."

"You want Brownie points?"

"No, I'm just saying…"

"Most newcomers," he said, "guys included, are emotional disasters by the time they get into recovery. Therefore they ought to be approached gently and cautiously. Usually, the better looking they are, the more together they seem to be, the less able they are to successfully navigate through a relationship."

"You should give some serious consideration to splitting up with Mercedes, Maestro. I think she's really a bad influence on you. You never used to come up with this stuff before you started hanging around with her."

"You remember where Edgar Cayce got all his information?"

"Cayce is also passe, Maestro. Off the radar."

"Just trying to make a point," said Tyler.

"Well, you'll have to get current if you want to score any points with the younger generation. The Keith Richards reference wasn't too bad, but you should mention somebody from Opie Gone Bad."

"...Opie Gone Bad?"

"Never mind...Aren't we getting a little off topic, Maestro? We started out with *Action is the magic word* and ended up with Edgar Cayce. A logical transition?"

"Maybe. But we're talking about action. What it is, what it does. And it's a natural segue into the Fourth Great Discovery—*Life works from the inside out.*"

"Where we can discuss your other favorite whacko, Teilhard de Chardin, who must have been reading Cayce when he came up with the idea of the Noosphere. I have this nightmare vision that soon we'll be researching Madam Blavatsky and the Theosophical Society."

"Hey, not a bad idea."

"I have to go to bed. All these high-altitude flights of fancy are giving me a nosebleed. I know what's going to happen next week, Tyler."

"You do?"

"I do. You're going to put all the responsibility for my life back on my shoulders. As if I wasn't dealt a crappy hand to start with, as if I was born with a silver spoon in my mouth...I didn't have it easy. You know that. Some people, like yours truly, had real difficulties, stuff that can't be dismissed with all this hocus pocus about Edgar Cayce and...the Noosphere and ...mind control. That kind of stuff only goes so far."

"You've got a minute left," said Tyler.

"...For what?"

"To finish your whine time. Remember? You only get three minutes a session. And you're..."

"I'm not whining, Tyler. I was merely trying to explain why all this is not as cut and dried as you would have me believe. There are variations of meanings, nuances, that seem to escape your sledge hammer approach. There is a responsibility to evaluate each..."

"Let me refer you to page ninety-seven in the Big Book...*Burn the idea into the consciousness of every man that he can get well regardless of anyone.* And the only condition, Edward?"

"...*That he trust God and clean house.*"

"And can trusting God and cleaning house be defined as actions?"

"Once again you've chosen to misinterpret my meaning and twist it into some devious form of logic that you think is..."

Right in the middle of the sentence he stands up, effectively terminating the meeting.

"I have to go," he said. "I promised Mercedes we'd go roller skating."

"...Roller skating?"

"Yeah...She wants to learn."

"*You* don't even know how to roller skate."

"I know that. But she doesn't. I mean doesn't know that I don't know...how to skate. So I'll just believe that I can and see what happens."

"Tyler..."

"Goodnight, Edward. Remember that I love you. And don't drink."

"I love you, too, Maestro...most of the time. But there are times when you can be a...burden."

"What is it they used to say? *If you love everybody at the meetings you're going to, you're not going to enough meetings.*"

"Probably true..." I said.

"So be of good cheer. All is well. I am a lesson, not a burden, Edward. I was sent to teach you things you would not ordinarily learn."

"I'll...take your word for it."

"And remember the Four Magic Words...Surrender control ...Accept responsibility."

"...Ugh..."

CHAPTER SEVEN

If you live in the desert, better learn to love the sand.
Anonymous

"How many more weeks, Maestro?"

"How many more weeks for what?"

"Till we're finished...with this. What we're doing."

"Well, we have this week for *Life works from the inside out*, then next week for *The more I rely on my Higher Power the more reliable it becomes* segment. Then we could perhaps do one or two of the Twelve Promises and maybe wind it up with a fear inventory or a conversation about Conditional Reality."

"That'll take a while, eh?"

"You have plans, Edward? Places you have to be that would preclude our meeting on a regular basis?"

"I have...or will have some...things that I have to take care of."

"A death in the family?...or just the demise of your moral compass?"

"...What a terrible thing to say."

"But accurate?"

"Of course not. For all you know there might be somebody very sick in my family."

"Besides you," he said.

"Tyler…You're so insensitive sometimes. Did you ever stop to think that there really might be somebody terribly sick in my family?"

"I did stop and think about that," he said. "Briefly. But then passed over it as not probable. The more realistic assessment was that you were planning some nefarious deed that you would rather not have me witness."

He just kills me. He never buys into the righteous indignation routine. Someday there really will be somebody sick and then I'll get to watch him fumble around trying to make amends.

"In my defense," I said, "I can't think of a single nefarious deed I have even in the planning stage."

"Let's do some free association. I'll say a word and you say the first thing that comes to mind."

"Okay."

"Drink."

"…Up."

"Bed."

"…Down."

"Sarah."

"Nefarious…Just kidding. Nefarious is too strong a word. It has connotations of evil. I have no evil intentions toward Sarah."

"The fact that you even have intentions toward Sarah has connotations of evil."

"My intentions are strictly honorable."

"Try to keep in mind that you are recently back in recovery after a relapse, and Pretty Sarah has very little sober time herself. That's not a good combination. You think you just waltz in after a relapse and continue on your way?

What's the sentence in the Big Book before the one about getting down to causes and conditions?"

"…Our liquor was but a symptom?"

"Right. So, even with all your knowledge about the program, you still had a relapse. Now is not the time to be getting into a relationship with a newcomer. She is sweet and she is wonderful, but it's bad for you and it's bad for her."

"Didn't you tell me that you dated one of your wives when she was only thirty days sober?"

"True," he said. "But just one date."

"What happened?"

"I realized that she was only thirty days sober. You have to understand that most people are basket cases when they first get sober."

"Sarah's been sober a lot longer than thirty days."

"But considerably less than a year."

"It doesn't say anything in the Big Book about not dating newcomers."

"It doesn't say anything about sponsorship either, but that's one of the strengths of the program, one of its unwritten suggestions. You know—*Get a sponsor; do the Steps.*"

"How'd you two end up getting married?"

"She invited me to her first-year birthday party," he said. "And the magic happened."

"Wouldn't happen today, Maestro. She wouldn't have been around after a year. Some Santa Monica lowrider would've scooped her up and waltzed her away before that first birthday. Things were different twenty-five years ago."

"Perhaps…But once again we are lost, far from our topic of the evening. I can't even remember what got us sidetracked."

"You accused me of plotting some nefarious deed having to do with Sarah."

"I remember. It was after you expressed concern that our weekly visits would go on past the mating season and you'd be left...doing without for the long winter months."

"No, I expressed my concern for a sick family member."

"And who might that be?"

"...Uncle Frank."

"He the one who was missing an ear?"

"That's him."

"Didn't you tell me he died a couple of years ago?"

"Did I...? Maybe it was Uncle Gene."

"Or maybe it was the Good Fairy," said Tyler. "I want you to do me a favor."

"Anything," I said.

"Carry a small notebook with you and make a notation every time you tell a lie."

"Just a small piece of paper will probably do."

"Try the notebook," he said. "You may be surprised at how many notations you make."

"How will I know if they're lies?"

"On second thought, make that a large notebook. And read The Doctor's Opinion in the front of the Big Book when you get a chance, especially the part about not being able to differentiate the true from the false."

"I was just kidding, Maestro. I know when I'm lying."

"Bourbon, seven, no ice?"

"You think that was a lie?" I said.

"One of the definitions of lying," said Tyler, "is, something meant to deceive or give the wrong impression."

"There was no attempt to deceive. *Bourbon, seven, no ice* is a simple, declarative sentence."

"Meant to deceive yourself into thinking you could have just one, or possibly two. But no more. The statement reeks of deception."

"I thought we didn't judge one another."

"I'm making a special exception in your case because you don't seem to realize the gravity of the situation. You're like, *Ho, Hum. Twelve years sober and I drank. Think I'll go hop in bed with Sarah.* May I suggest you're looking for a distraction rather than a solution."

"No…"

"Yes. You're looking for something Out There to make you feel Okay. So we try various things: whiskey, sex, food, gambling, other things, substances or behaviors meant to fill that space…And so, as Fate would have it, we come full circle to the topic: *Life works from the inside out.*"

"What do we do now that we're there?" I said.

"You believe it?"

"I'm not sure I know what it means."

"It means that Life is an inside job," he said. "Really an inside job."

"…So?"

"So it's not happening *out there*, which is what our senses tell us. But then our senses are lovely liars. It's happening *in here*, and being projected *out there*. Think movies."

"What is it that's happening…*in here*?"

"Life…"

"I'm not thinking movies; I'm thinking that you've finally gone over the edge, Maestro."

"Listen to this:

In your system of reality you are learning what mental energy is and how to use it. You do this by constantly transforming your thoughts and emotions into physical reality. You are supposed to get a clear picture of your inner development by perceiving the exterior environment. What seems to be a perception...is instead the materialization of our inner emotions, energy and mental environment..."

"...Houdini?"

"From the Seth Material."

"That sound you hear is the last of your loyal fans heading for the exits."

"Wait, it gets better," said Tyler. *"Classical* physics tells us that there's a real world *out there,* independent of human consciousness."

"...You're saying there isn't?"

"Wait, O Eager One. Yet *Quantum* physics tells us that consciousness itself is deeply and inextricably involved in the world that we think of as being *out there.*"

"And just what does all that mean?"

"For one thing, it may mean that life actually does work from the inside out, that we are possibly co-creators, partners in this mystery we call life."

"Partners with who?"

"With whom..." said Tyler.

"Stop already. You know what I mean."

"You know who David Bohm is?"

"The physicist?"

"He talks about the Implicate Order, the underlying order, the unmanifest aspect of reality, outside space-time."

"So you think this Implicate Order is another name for God?"

"I think of it as kind of a Divine Soup," said Tyler.

"I don't like soup. Or salad."

"That's one reason you're not very healthy," he said.

"You're the one who's not healthy. You're the one who has hot dogs and root beer floats for breakfast."

"I have never had a root beer float for breakfast...A Pepsi float maybe."

"Jesus..." I can only shake my head.

"So what if this Divine Soup," he said, "this reservoir of Order, contained all the information you'd ever need to make decisions, to build things, to invent new things...make a better world?"

"Then I'd certainly order a large bowl and a big spoon. But what if it was a trap, like the Garden of Eden thing?"

"How was the Garden of Eden a trap?" said Tyler.

"Clearly, Maestro. A sting, if you will, by the Almighty Himself. God sets up this scenario where he tells Adam and Eve not to eat the fruit of a certain tree because if they do they shall be as gods, knowing good and evil. How could they resist? An obvious case of entrapment."

"I thought the Snake told them that."

"Maybe God and the Snake were in cahoots. Who knows? All I know is that any decent lawyer could have gotten Adam and Eve off with a warning—a simple case of mistaken tree identity. House arrest at most. Instead they get banished from Paradise for life. Then we *all* get banished for life. How fair is that?"

"Well," said Tyler, "I wouldn't take the Bible story too literally."

"That's not what I heard," I said.

"That's because you took Brother Eagan's Religion One class when you were young and impressionable. It's meant as an allegory, a myth, a story about creation. All cultures have stories about creation...and they're all different. It's mostly a matter of geography—what story you get is determined by where you were born. If you were born in Baghdad you got a different story than the guy who was born in Kansas City."

"...Who decides who's got the right story?"

"We have wars over that exact question," said Tyler. "Turns out that everyone gets to decide for themselves, though there are sometimes elements of coercion on young minds. Trouble is, when they decide, they want to decide for everybody else, too. They want *you* to believe *their* creation story."

"And if I don't?

"They want to kill you."

"Why would they want to do that?" I said.

"I'm not sure anybody really knows."

"The guys who want to kill me must know."

"Don't be too sure," said Tyler. "Deeply imbedded in the soul of every religious fanatic is the heartfelt need to destroy all the infidels. Infidels being defined as people who believe other things...than they believe. Doesn't have to make sense."

"Crazy, eh?"

"But let's get back to the *Life works from the inside out,*" said Tyler. "Where were we?"

"I think we were on the verge of slurping up some Divine Soup."

"Right," he said. "It's the Implicate Order, the Storehouse of Miracles waiting to happen, waiting to be dragged off the Shelf and made manifest in our paltry three-dimensional world."

"So how do we get access to this Implicate thing?" I said. "What's the key?"

"For the key we have to turn to the mystic. It's only then that we realize that both the mystic and the physicist have encountered an underlying, multidimensional reality."

"Let's cut to the chase. How do we get to the Storehouse of Miracles? I'm badly in need of a miracle."

"Sarah?"

"Who else?"

"You're not going to like the answer," said Tyler.

"Just give it to me. I'll decide whether I like it or not."

"The answer...is prayer. Meditation"

"You're right," I said, "I don't like it."

"You're allowed not to like it."

"That's the only way? Prayer?"

"I call it prayer, but you could use other terms."

"You know how nervous I get about prayer...And now I have to start worrying about those people who want to kill me because I don't believe in their prayers. I'm neutral. I don't believe in *anybody's* prayers."

"The mystic searches for an inner wisdom," said Tyler, reading from his notebook but pretending not to, "reached through an altered state of consciousness. This altered state is similar to the Implicate Order in that it...aligns one with the wholeness of reality. Think Step Eleven."

"Was I asleep during the 'wholeness of reality' lecture?"

"The 'wholeness of reality' lecture followed the 'ground of Being' lecture."

"I must have slept in that whole day," I said.

"We'll go slowly...Some of it has to do with Jung's Collective Unconscious where all humanity gathers nightly for a Town Meeting. Then there's the *pleroma,* the potential..."

"Overload! Overload!" I said, raising both hands. "My Inner Child just developed a migraine headache."

"Enough for today?"

"Did you see the Bachooki light up?"

"And what, pray tell, is a Bachooki?" he said.

"It's an electromagnetic device designed to detect bullshit …and suddenly all the warning lights are on."

"That must be our signal to sign off for the night."

"Thank you, Maestro. And goodnight."

"Sleep well…And give your Inner Child a cookie. That often helps."

"…Good night, Maestro."

CHAPTER EIGHT

God is bound to act, to pour Himself into thee
as soon as He shall find thee ready.
                    Meister Eckhart

"And so we come to the last Great Discovery," he said.
"Which is...?"

"*The more I rely on my Higher Power, the more reliable*
It becomes. I hope this isn't going to be another circus...like
last week's session."

"What was so...circusy about last week's session."

"It was goofy. Too much information that people can't
use. Nobody's going to remember all that stuff about the
Implicate Order, or Quantum Physics."

"It was meant to reinforce the idea," he said, "that there
are more fish in this interior ocean than we imagine, more
miracles waiting to be discovered. That indeed *Life does*
work from the inside out, hence the emphasis on the Third
and Eleventh Steps."

"Well, it didn't do any of that. You know, all that
marvelous, logical information you have tucked away in
your head, doesn't always come out in the orderly fashion
that you think it does."

"...It doesn't?"

"...Not always."

"I could be arrested for disorderly thinking?" he said.

"Possibly…You'd need a good lawyer."

"Good thing we know a couple. Be a slam-dunk with the two of them. If they could beat the Big Guy on the Garden of Eden sting, they shouldn't have any trouble getting me off on a Disorderly Thinking rap. I'll make an effort to be less…obtuse."

"The few fans you have left will appreciate the effort."

"So, back to the Discovery," he said. "…The more I rely on this Power, et cetera…"

"How do you know it's true…The more you rely on this Power, the more reliable It becomes?"

"Like all the things I've learned in recovery—trial and error."

"I mean how do you tell that It's becoming more reliable? Your Higher Power. You know, like what criteria do you use?"

"…What criteria do I use?" said Tyler.

"Don't stall, Maestro. You heard the question."

He fiddled with that little wheel on his hearing aid to indicate his difficulty with hearing. But, as you can imagine, I wasn't fooled.

"…The results," he said finally.

"I thought we weren't supposed to be in the results business."

"…Semantics, Noble Student."

"This is Word Games 101?"

"Edward…Please note in the manuscript that there is a hint of exasperation in my voice."

"Done," I said….(*Maestro exasperated!*)

"This is not doing something in order to obtain a certain result. This is doing something and observing the outcome. The result…without attachment."

"Exasperation noted, Maestro. So what results are we talking about?"

"The results of my experiments."

"And just what experiments did you conduct?"

"I tried praying…and not praying," said Tyler. "Although that's not exactly the same thing as relying and not relying."

"And the results were?"

"You know, you're beginning to sound like me."

"Frightening thought," I said. "Did you ever pray for things? Maybe for hot babes in your younger years?"

"I did some of that," he said. "I also prayed that I wouldn't wake up in the morning, so I could go straight to heaven where the streets were paved with gold. Though for the life of me I can't imagine why I thought streets of gold would be wonderful. My mother told me that. And…I prayed that my father would die."

"You think that's a good prayer?" I said. "I mean the one about your father."

"I didn't judge it…I just said it. I didn't know how else to get rid of him."

"You thought he was the source of your problems? Or your troubles as it says in the Big Book."

"I did," he said.

"But he wasn't."

"No. Of course not. Sadly enough, I was the source of my troubles. You remember: Selfishness, self-centeredness."

"I'd have to call that a low rent prayer, Maestro."

"Well, I don't see it as one of my finer moments," he said.

"Did your prayer get answered?"

"Eventually."

"Does that count as part of the reliance thing?" I said.

"No...Because he would have died eventually anyway. I was just trying to speed up the process."

"...That's the coldest thing I've ever heard you say."

"I say it once in awhile to remind myself that I haven't yet arrived at some pinnacle of spirituality."

"But that didn't really count as part of the experiment."

"No. It was too soon for me to have any frame of reference about prayer," he said. "But you must have prayed at one time. All Catholic kids do...mainly because we're terrified not to—the fires of Hell are constantly licking at our feet, fueled by the vision of the many sins we were actually committing or would like to commit."

"I learned about Novenas in high school," I said. "You know, specific prayers for a certain number of days to obtain favors from the Almighty."

"I remember."

"Well, first thing I did was say a Novena hoping to lure Melinda Marlowe into the back seat of my car."

"Did somebody mention low rent?" he said.

"This was a very innocent request. Not like praying that someone would die."

"Did it work?" he said.

"Not for a couple of years," I said. "And then it was a different girl."

"So would you say that was an instance of your Higher Power being reliable?"

"You're the one with this thing about reliability, Maestro. Besides, we seem to be interchanging the terms. Are prayer and reliance the same thing?"

93

"Prayer, at least as it's usually understood, is a reverent petition to God. But then there are different kinds of prayers, like the prayer of thanksgiving, the prayer of devotion, the well-known gimme prayer...and others."

"And reliance?" I said.

"Reliance implies a certain level of confidence, trust... dependence even. If I had to pick a word, I'd say trust."

"So," I said, "the more I trust this Higher Power, the more trustworthy It becomes?"

"Right. And more accessible. The trust is a reminder that you're safe, that you're always connected to this Power, that help is only a prayer, or a thought, away. Always, whether it seems like it or not. Keep that in mind."

"How?"

"Lots of ways," he said. "Conscious contact. You could go down to the Beads and Bangles store, get twelve medium-size beads and string them together. Like a mini-rosary. Then when you're driving around, you could turn off Sport's Talk Radio once in a while and get in touch with your Higher Power."

"...And just how do I go about getting in touch with my Higher Power using these beads?"

"You get out the string of beads you just made and say one of the Steps on each bead. Or say the Jesus Prayer."

"I'm not into Jesus," I said.

"Nothing wrong with Jesus," said Tyler. "It's the Christians you have to be careful of. Or...you could just repeat the names of God."

"What are some of the names?" I said.

"Actually, G-o-d would work. Krishna. Allah. Big Thunder. What have we been doing for the last twelve years? How many times have we talked about this?"

"Lots of times," I said. "I mean I listened, but…It was like those exercises I was supposed to do for my back when I screwed it up. I listened to the physical therapist, took the instructions home and put them in a drawer."

"And never did them."

"Once or twice."

"So that's why it took so long for your back to heal."

"Maybe."

"No maybe about it," said Tyler. "This is about action, Edward. Taking the information and filing it in some… mental cabinet isn't good enough. You're going to have to *do* something."

"Well, I don't know how to do Reliance-on-a-Higher-Power."

"How do you work the Third Step?"

"I…make a decision to turn my will and my life over. I read the words. I say them. But…"

"But what?" he said.

"Is that doing it? Isn't there something else? How do I know if I've really done it?"

"Short answer is you don't," he said. "You say the words and trust, believe, have faith that Some-one or Some-thing is listening."

"…I think that's dumb."

"That why you don't do it?"

"Oh, I do it, Tyler. I do it."

"Sometimes," he said.

"Right. I do it some-times. But it doesn't do any good. Trust me. What are five failed marriages, a ball-breaker job at Safeway and a hundred and thirty-two rejection slips supposed to add up to? This is the Broad Highway of Success? The result of twelve years of meetings and service work?"

"You had sobriety," he said.

"Sobriety for what—to be miserable? Besides, doesn't it say somewhere that we feel a man unthinking when he says that sobriety is enough."

"It does say that, but it says that in conjunction with the ninth step, the middle of the amends process. It means that a mumbled *I'm sorry* won't get it. It's an action process. We have to go out and make amends for the harm done."

"...I'm not happy, Tyler."

"So?"

"So I'm not happy...and I'd like to *be* happy."

"Everybody'd like to be happy," said Tyler.

"I thought sobriety would help me to be happy."

"Sometimes it does...But being in recovery only means that you're in recovery. The happy part is up to you."

"And I'm mad at God. Really mad."

"You tell Him that? Or Her."

"...No...Seems too dangerous," I said.

"That's a mouthful for somebody who professes not to believe in God."

"I'm not taking any unnecessary risks, Tyler. On the off chance that there really is a God, I think I owe it to myself to be careful. I've read the stories. God makes toast out of people who piss Him off. He smites people. Big time."

"People smite people," said Tyler.

"...But God sends them—the people who are the smiters. Don't kid yourself. Remember Lot's Wife? She got turned into a pillar of salt, just for turning around and looking at the city they were leaving. A pillar of *salt*, Tyler. Just for looking."

"Pardon the pun, but you should take all those stories with a grain of salt."

"...Besides, if God knows everything, why do we have to spend time telling Him what we think of Him, how we love Him, or what we want? Or thanking Him for my latest divorce? Or the last ten rejection slips."

"I'm not sure why," he said. "It's one of those W words I try to avoid. The best I can do is believe that it's part of the deal. It's our participation in the process. And, as someone told me one bleak night, it will be necessary for me to participate in my own recovery."

"So if I'm mad at God, I should tell Him?"

"Absolutely. Yell at Him if you want to. Use the F word. Use lots of four-letter words. Throw in a couple of twelve-letter words. My personal opinion is that you're never closer to God than when you're being honest. If you think God sucks, tell Him. If you think life's a bad deal, let Him know."

"You're guaranteeing that I won't be struck by lightning? Or turned into a pillar of salt?"

"You have my personal guarantee," he said.

"What if I am?"

"Why must you always go to the worst possible scenario? Chances of getting hit by lightning have got to be millions to one. Or better. Yet that's the thing you think about."

"For one thing, I'm not so sure this Power is all that reliable."

"Which brings us back to our discovery," he said.

"...I'm treading water, Maestro. My life preserver is water logged. I'm slowly sinking."

"Trust, Edward. Trust."

"Easy for you to say. You're not in danger of sinking."

"We're all in danger of sinking, Edward. You know that. There's no safe place. No mountain top where we finally get to rest."

"…I'd really like to have a drink," I said, not sure if I meant it or not.

"Tomorrow," said Tyler. "Plenty of time tomorrow to have a drink. In the meantime, think of something for next week. Maybe one of the twelve promises. Or maybe something from Walt Whitman."

"What if I did both?" I said.

"That would be acceptable."

"Will next week be our last week?" I said.

"…It depends."

"On what? On whether you get lucky with Mercedes?"

"No luck involved," he said. "She won't leave me alone. Sex, sex and more sex. It's all she thinks about. She's driving me crazy."

"…Tyler."

He stared off in space for a few moments before he spoke.

"You know, you should read more books," he said.

"What kind of books did you have in mind, Maestro? Comic books, self-help books, cook books…?"

"I think books about God would be best. Try Winnie the Pooh, Star Wars, Dr. Seuss…"

"Those are kids' books."

"I know," he said. "They're always about God."

I was beginning to worry about him; he still had that same thousand-yard stare.

"You might want to scan the Big Book," he said, "and the Twelve and Twelve, plus Language of the Heart, The Tao of Physics, and anything else you have lying around. Maybe some Peanuts cartoons."

"You okay?" I said.

He looked at me like the question was a surprise.

"Yeah. I'm fine."

"That's a lot of stuff to read in a week. I haven't even found a book of poems by Bukowski."

"Try Burning in Water, Drowning in Flames."

"You know," I said, "I'm beginning to think that you don't want to finish this book. Ever. You just want it to go on and on and on. That way, I'll be like an indentured servant, forever kneeling at the feet of The Master."

He didn't respond for a few moments.

Then:

"Where did that come from, Edward?"

"...I don't know."

"Can we call that a resentment?"

"Possibly..."

"And I'm the cause?" he said.

"...I think so."

"What have I done to cause all this...discomfort in your life?"

I was as surprised by my outburst as he probably was. Truth is, I didn't know if he had done anything to cause it. It just came out that way.

"...Oh...I don't know. I'm just angry all the time."

"At me?" he said.

I just shrugged.

"And underneath the anger?"

"Probably fear, I said.

"Fear of?"

"...Everything. I just want to hide. I don't want to *do* all this again, Tyler. All this newcomer shit. The goddam Steps, the meetings, the pep rally atmosphere...the whole thing. I'm tired of *you* treating me like a newcomer. I've got twelve years in recovery. Twelve. I'm not a newcomer. Not really."

"Granted. You are simply encouraged to admit to the relapse and get on with your life. The lesson is for you and for others."

"I wish I'd never told anyone," I said.

"You think you'd feel better?"

"…You know, I wanted to be your replacement. Wanted to be Tyler after you…retired. Might as well say it—after you died. Now I'll have to wait maybe fifteen more years. I'll be sixty-five, for chrissakes."

"Sixty-five is not a fatal age, Edward."

"It won't be the same. You'll be dead and I won't be ready. Sometimes I just want to pack it in."

"We place way too much emphasis on time in recovery," he said, "like the more time you've got, the smarter you are."

"Well," I said. "That's certainly not true in your case."

"It's not true in anybody's case."

"People probably don't know that you're having sex with a seventy-year-old vampire…and that you're secretly smoking while pretending not to. If you want to know the truth, I don't think you're all that well."

"I never claimed to be well, Edward. Just sober. Well is a moving target. Trouble is, once I make getting well a goal, it turns out I can never get well enough."

"Everybody thinks you're a goddam prince."

"I'll gladly disown the title."

"People actually love and respect you."

"…Sometimes it can't be helped," he said.

"I'm a little embarrassed to admit it, but I want people to love and respect me, too."

"Nothing to be embarrassed about. Love and respect are nice…You think it will make you happy? Being loved and respected?"

"I *do* think that," I said.

"Don't forget the lesson about *Life works from the inside out.*"

"I know, but maybe I can jump start the routine by getting a little love and respect first...*then* get the insides working."

"There are plenty of people who love and respect you. I know of only one person who doesn't feel that way about you."

"Who's that?"

"You."

"Ah, Tyler. I give up."

"If only I could believe that."

"...You know I was thrown out of the Boy Scouts when I was eleven."

"I didn't know that," he said "What happened?"

"They have this thing where you walk fifty paces, then jog fifty paces, and you have to do a mile in twelve minutes, plus or minus something."

"How'd you do?"

"Twelve minutes, right on the money."

"And the problem was?"

"I had a watch."

"That was a no-no?" he said.

"Apparently. They called it cheating. I tried to explain that I didn't have any way of knowing if I should walk faster or jog slower unless I had a watch. But they failed to grasp the logic."

"They probably had not had the benefit of your training in Advanced Logic."

"Ahhh..."

"So, in order to facilitate this process of relying on G-o-d, buy some small Avery stickers, write something like

STEP#3 on one of them and stick it on your watch face. Then, every time you look at your watch you'll be reminded about the decision to turn your will and your life over to... Something."

"God..." I said

"What's the definition of insanity?" he said.

"Doing the same thing over and over and expecting different results."

"I rest my case."

"Finally," I said.

"...And to all a good night," as he got up to leave.

"Goodnight, Maestro. I'm sorry for the outburst."

"Nothing to be sorry for. I'm glad it happened. Once you can acknowledge it, whatever it is, you can deal with it. It's the secrets that kill us, the unwillingness to share the darkness, the isolation, and the hideous sense of separation."

"I'll be ready for next week."

"I know you will. Goodnight, Edward."

CHAPTER NINE

*Can you walk on water? You have done no better
than a straw. Can you fly in the air? You have done
no better than a sparrow. Conquer your heart; then
you may become somebody.*

Ansari of Heart

"I was into one of the books you suggested I read and this
guy said that Classical Physics sees the world as a machine
and Quantum Physics sees it as an idea."

"You buy it?" said Tyler.

"I'm not sure what it means."

"My interpretation is that if it's a machine, it's impervious
to outside influences, impenetrable, inaccessible, sealed,
closed, ...and so forth."

"Further explanation required, Boss."

"If we take the mechanistic approach," he said, "it leads
to the belief that this universe that we know, this Machine
if you will, was set in motion billions of years ago and is
relentlessly grinding its way to extinction, to entropy. Turns
out you're just a passenger on a doomed ship."

"And if it's an idea?" I said.

"If it's an idea, then maybe we exist in the Mind of God,
which may lead you to believe that everything's alive, that all
things are possible, that it's all connected, and that everything

effects everything else. Life is Whole Cloth. Einstein said that the sense of separation we feel is an illusion."

"Which brings us back to...everything we say, do, or think makes a difference."

"Ah, you just get smarter by the day," he said.

"Don't I wish."

"You come up with anything to discuss?" he said.

"Lots of things."

"Like?"

"Oh, the disconnect I often feel, some of the Promises, Walt Whitman, especially the preface to Leaves of Grass..."

"And the lie you told yourself before you took a drink?"

"That, too," I said.

"Do Whitman first, that should get us in the mood. You've got it written down?"

"Right here in my trusty notebook. You want to hear it?"

"I do."

"Here it is...most of it anyway:

This is what you shall do: Love the earth and the sun and the animals, despise riches, give alms to everyone that asks, stand up for the stupid and the crazy, devote your income and labor to others, hate tyrants, argue not concerning God, have patience and indulgence toward the people...go freely with powerful uneducated persons and with the young and the mothers of families, reexamine all you have been told at school or church or in any book, dismiss whatever insults your soul, and your very flesh shall be a great poem...

"I've always liked the, *argue not concerning God* part."

"Me, too," I said. "I wonder why we find it necessary to argue about God? What difference does it make?"

104

"I have a feeling," he said, "that that's why they put *God as we understood Him* in the Big Book."

"And the part where somebody, I think Ebby, says, *Why don't you choose your own conception of God?*"

"What did you think when you first read that?"

"It almost seemed like cheating," I said. "Like what we were told the Protestants were doing, twisting the original Word to suit themselves...Somehow it didn't seem real. I mean how could you just pick anything to be your Higher Power and actually have It be a Higher Power. What if I picked the moon?"

"Okay. What if you did?" he said.

"The moon can't be my Higher Power, Tyler. That's ridiculous. It's just a round rock off in space somewhere."

"You'd be a moon worshipper. And not the first by the way."

"The people who worshipped the moon were primitives. They didn't have a clue about what the moon really was. We had sun worshippers, too. But that doesn't mean the sun's God."

"You think it worked for them?" said Tyler.

"...I don't know what *worked for them* means."

"Do you think they were comforted by the thought that the sun was protecting them?"

"They made human sacrifices to the sun, Tyler. That's barbaric, for chrissakes. Young chicks. Virgins yet. They were savages. They didn't know anything."

"At one time," he said, "lots of very bright people thought the earth was flat...and that the sun and the planets revolved around the earth."

"So?"

"So it isn't about being smart. Making sacrifices to the Sun God made people feel secure, like Someone or Something was watching over them, protecting them."

"They were bribing God," I said. *"Gimme another virgin, Frank.* Making sure the Rain God would bring water for the crops and that the sun would do its job. We're back to fear again."

"What else?" he said. "Do you think you have to know what God is, or who God is, before you can believe?"

"It says, *God as you understand Him.* Implying that you have some...knowledge of this...this thing you're turning your will and your life over to."

"I've often thought they should reword that to say, God as you do or don't understand Him."

"Now you want to rewrite the Big Book."

"Just a comment. Understanding, meaning something you can define, is not required. What I want to suggest is that you give some thought to the part in the Book that says something like...*as soon as a man is even willing to believe, we emphatically assure him that he is on his way.*"

"On his way...to see the Wizard?"

"Maybe...You believed once."

"I did."

"What happened?"

"...I don't know."

"Dig a little," said Tyler.

"One day I was at Mass and it occurred to me that I didn't believe anymore. Out of the blue. Not in religion, and certainly not in God...But I was afraid not to believe."

"Fear again?" said Tyler.

106

"Sure fear. What if God got one of His henchmen to smite me? So I kept going to church, knowing it was a sham, but not knowing what else to do."

"But eventually you stopped going," he said.

"I did. And then I got very angry with this God I didn't believe in because I had wasted all that time going to church, saying prayers to someone who turned out to be like the guy behind the curtain in the Wizard of Oz."

"That was the Wizard himself," said Tyler.

"I know that, but he turns out to be a fraud."

"No. He turns out to be a very wise Wizard who sends Dorothy and her companions off on a quest in order to show them that they already possess the qualities they had come to get from him. And after the quest he gives them each something that symbolizes what they thought they were missing."

"Like what?" I said.

"The Scarecrow gets a diploma as a Doctor of Thinkology, the Lion gets a Medal of Valor, and the Tinman gets a Heart-Shaped Watch...You see, there isn't anything to *get*, there is only something to *be*."

"...And just what is it that I might be, O Wizardly One?" I said.

"You are a Child of the Universe, loved and cherished by this Power you don't believe in. No need to justify your existence. *Being* is its own reward."

"Let's go over it one more time, Maestro. If all that is true, why don't I feel like I'm loved and cherished by this Teddy Bear God of yours?"

"You're so busy judging yourself, chastising yourself for real or imagined faults, trying to become a Better Person, that you've left very little space where love can enter. There is no better to get, Edward. But it's all conditional for you—*I'll be loved when I lose twenty pounds, bench press two-fifty, get a better job*, et cetera. Your capacity to receive love is always put at some distant point."

"...*Dismiss whatever insults your soul*, eh?" I said.

"*And your very flesh shall be a great poem*," said Tyler.

"I don't think that can happen, Maestro. For you, maybe, but not for me. My relapse puts me into another category."

"And what category might that be, Edward?"

"The...less-deserving category."

"You know which one of the Promises is my favorite?"

"...No."

"*That feeling of uselessness and self-pity will disappear.*"

"But you haven't relapsed, Maestro. I think I automatically placed myself in one of the Lower Circles of Hell when I took a drink."

"Next time you go to a meeting ask how many people stayed sober from their first meeting. You won't see many hands go up."

"But you did," I said.

"For years that's what I claimed, but it isn't true. I went to my first meeting when I was twenty-two years old, locked up on the Honor Farm for what they used to call drunk driving. I went to a meeting because somebody told me I'd get three days good time if I went."

"And...?"

"I didn't get the three days good time so I stopped going. The next time I went it was nine years later and I was in jail again. I didn't want what you had. I had no intention of getting sober. None. I went to meetings because I wanted to get out of the cellblock at night."

"What happened?"

108

"One night I heard a guy say, *If you're waiting to get better you can stop waiting because you'll never be any better than you are right now.*"

"Heavy duty," I said.

"At first I thought it was a really stupid thing to say. But the more I thought about it, the more it made sense. Then I heard another guy say, *If you're not happy today, chances are you won't be happy tomorrow.*"

"Meaning?"

"Meaning that I should stop putting my life on hold, get out of the results business, and stop waiting for some future fantasy to arrive. *Now* is the time, *here* is the place. It's very Biblical ...*Rejoice and be glad, for this is the day the Lord has made.*"

"Want to hear my favorite Promise?"

"Shoot," he said.

"*We will comprehend the word serenity and we will know peace*...I'd love to have that one come true."

"And you don't think it could?" he said.

"Sometimes I think I just want out, Maestro. Still. That's all. I don't want to think. I don't want to be afraid. I don't want to argue about anything. I just don't want to *be* anymore."

"Serenity comes to me when I'm not thinking about myself. Contrary to popular myth, Alcoholics Anonymous is not a self-help program. It's an *other*-help program. The peace and serenity will come when you stop chasing it and let it catch up to you."

"You're aware, of course, that what you just said doesn't make a bit of sense."

"I am. But that's the secret behind the *koan*, a problem impossible to solve with the intellect. The intellect knocks itself out trying to figure-it-out. Got that? Figure-It-Out."

109

"Don't keep me in suspense, Maestro."

"So the intellect eventually gives up just this side of madness and despair, and another of the Promises kicks in. The question to you is—Which one?"

"*We will intuitively know how to handle situations which used to baffle us.*"

"Bravo, counselor...Intuitively."

"I think I'm at the madness and despair stage," I said.

"A necessary place to be," said Tyler. "The intellect, the figure-it-out part, eventually gives up because it becomes convinced it can't find a solution. That allows the intuitive part to enter."

"...And...?"

"Find a solution," he said.

"Intuitively," I said.

"Eventually," he said.

"...I'm confused and filled with despair."

"Let it sink in. Time will supply what's missing. Now for the final question. What was the lie you told yourself before you took a drink?"

"I think it was...I can have just one. And Just-One will quiet the Demons."

"Did you know it was a lie when you said it?"

"I don't know, Tyler. You think I evaluate these things in the moment? Have them come to mind and play True or False? I just knew I was going to go absolutely insane if I didn't do something."

"And a drink seemed like the quickest way to...to what?"

"To quiet the voices...to somehow survive the madness and despair. I didn't think it through. They always say that... *Think it through before you take a drink.* But I wanted, needed a drink more than I needed to think it through. More than I needed anything. You know what that's like."

"I do."

"I didn't *care* what happened. Just give me a drink. Right now. One or two is all I need. Get the monkey off my back. That's the lie. That I could have one or two and then quit."

"But once you activate the craving…"

"Yeah…It's all over, isn't it?"

"It is. Then, if you're lucky, you start the long climb back into recovery. A climb that's much harder than the first one. The first time, there are elements of hope that keep you going. The second, third, tenth time, that starry-eyed wonder is gone. It's truly trudging, filled with doubt, wondering, after all those years, what happened."

"What did I do wrong?"

"Stay out of the right and wrong business, Edward. Your natural state, as an alcoholic, is to be drinking. You had twelve years of living in an unnatural condition of being sober."

"But why, Maestro? What could have possessed me to take a drink?"

"A quick survey reveals that you cut down on your meetings and were doing less service work. That's a good place to start. You see, something happens at meetings that transcends our ability to put it into words. Some kind of spiritual energy permeates the atmosphere. But I have to *be there* to experience it."

"Something happens?" I said.

"Right. I approach the Great Unknown, with my heart in my hands, and ask God to take it. The heart, which has just been ripped out of my chest and lies beating in my hands"

"That's how it has to be?"

111

"It is," he said. "You tear your heart out, give it to God, and are assured that this Higher Power will assign portions of it to others who need the life-giving nourishment of recovery. You remember—it's a language of the heart."

"God, I don't understand!"

"Understanding not required, Edward. Only action is required. Understanding will come later, when you don't feel the need for it."

"Then I'll be able to explain to others how it happens," I said.

"No," he said. "It will forever lay beyond words that we know. You can only demonstrate it. The others will know and follow your example. Someday, when more people walk the path, we will have the vocabulary, but not now."

"Tell me I'm not going insane."

"You're not going insane," he said.

"…You just said that because I asked you to say it."

"No, I said it because it's true."

"I don't want to go through this every few years, Tyler. This…madness."

"When was the last time?"

"Oh…a few years ago."

"You were five. The Dark Night. So it was seven years ago."

"So it happens every seven years?" I said.

"It happens…when it happens. No timetable."

"I can't do another one like this, Maestro. It'll kill me."

"As they say, *Only the good die young*."

"…You have never been less comforting," I said.

"Not my job to be comforting. It's my job to offer experience, strength and hope. And to tell you the truth."

"...You're going to suggest that I go back to the Rusty Zipper Group. Aren't you?"

"Actually I was," he said.

"You remember I wasn't so successful with Father Eddy."

"Your job is to carry the message, not the alcoholic. Some people can hear it; some can't. Not your job to decide."

"...You know, I can't make it without the Community."

"Few of us can," he said.

"I'll see you around?"

"You will."

"I'm told you're playing the ponies again, Maestro."

"Bless the Recovery Rumor Mill," he said.

"True?" I persisted.

"I have made some small wagers on a few of what I mistakenly believed were speedy nags."

"Successfully?"

"Indulge me, Edward. Let me have a few vices to flavor my old age. The designers of low-rise jeans have helped to brighten my remaining days. I have surely earned more than bread and water."

"You have earned the love and respect of the Community."

"And they have earned my eternal gratitude for the life they have given me."

"So what's next for you, Maestro?"

"I'm told that Hollywood is interested in some of the stuff we've done."

"My name up in lights as the author?"

"Possibly...But first, off to the Rusty Zipper Group and see if you can't find somebody interested in a sponsor."

"My name up in lights," I repeated.

"Edward Bear," he said, "in four-foot letters."

"...I can't use my real name?"

"No…Anonymity issues."

"Doesn't seem fair," I said. "All this time and…"

"What we want is mercy, not justice…or fairness. Just mercy."

"Stay alive, Maestro. I may need you in the near future. At least until my future in Hollywood is assured."

"I can work it from both sides of the Veil," he said.

"I need you on *this* side."

"Then I'll be there."

"Goodnight."

"Can I use your phone? I have to call Mercedes."

"…You're the best, Maestro."

"Ain't I though."

ABOUT THE AUTHOR

Edward Bear was born in Brooklyn, grew up in Los Angeles, and had a lifetime love affair with baseball. After a brief stint in the minor leagues followed by years in dead-end jobs, he worked at Hewlett-Packard for nearly thirty years. Mr. Bear lived high up in the Rocky Mountains with his wife, played a vintage Martin guitar, and wrote in the time the gods and goddesses gave him. Though he passed away in 2006, his words and wisdom live on.

To learn more about Mr. Bear, visit edwardbear.net or edwardbear01@gmail.com